THOMAS MÜNTZER

———— *A Tragedy of Errors* ————

THOMAS MÜNTZER

ERIC W. GRITSCH

FORTRESS PRESS   **MINNEAPOLIS**

1989

Thomas Müntzer:
A Tragedy of Errors

Book Design and Cover Design by Publisher's WorkGroup, Inc.

Library of Congress Cataloging-in-Publication Data

Gritsch, Eric W.
  Thomas Müntzer, a tragedy of errors / Eric W. Gritsch.
    p. cm.
  Bibliography: p.
  Includes index.
  ISBN 0–8006–0907–7
  1. Müntzer, Thomas, 1490 (ca.)–1525. 2. Reformation—Germany–
–Biography. 3. Radicals—Germany—Biography. I. Title.
BX4946.M8G73 1989
284'.3'092—dc20   89–12032
[B]

The paper used in this publication meets the minimum requirements of American National Standard for Information Sciences— Permanence of Paper for Printed Library Materials, ANSI Z39.48-1984.   ∞™

Manufactured in the U.S.A.   AF 1-907
93   92   91   90   89   1   2   3   4   5   6   7   8   9   10

CONTENTS

ABBREVIATIONS

AGBM   *Akten zur Geschichte des Bauernkriegs in Mittel-*
            deutschland. Vol. 1,1. Ed. Otto Merx. Vol. 1,2. Ed.
            Günther Franz. Leipzig, 1923–1934. Vol 2. Ed. W. P.
            Fuchs. Jena, 1942. Reprint, Aalen: Scientia, 1964.

ARG   *Archiv für Reformationsgeschichte.*

E   Elliger, Walter. *Thomas Müntzer. Leben und Werk.*
            Göttingen, W. Ger.: Vandenhoeck & Ruprecht, 1975.

HZ   *Zeitschrift des Harzvereins für Geschichte und Alter-*
            tumskunde. Continued as *Harz-Zeitschrift für den*
            Harzverein.

KD   *Kerygma und Dogma.*

LJ   *Luther-Jahrbuch*

LC   Smith, Preserved, and Charles M. Jacobs, eds.
            Luther's Correspondence. 2 vols. Philadelphia:
            Muhlenberg Press, 1913–18.

LW   *Luther's Works.* U.S. ed. 55 vols. Ed. Jaroslav Pelikan
            and Helmut Lehmann. Philadelphia: Fortress Press;
            St. Louis: Concordia Publishing House, 1955–86.

MSB   *Thomas Müntzer. Schriften und Briefe.* Kritische
            Gesamtausgabe. Quellen und Forschungen zur Refor-
            mationsgeschichte. Vol. 33. Ed. Günther Franz.
            Gütersloh, W. Ger.: Gerd Mohn, 1968.

SCJ   *The Sixteenth Century Journal.*

St.L   *D. Martin Luthers Sämmtliche Schriften.* 2d ed., ed.
            Johann Georg Walch. 23 vols. St. Louis, 1890–1910.

TL   *Theologische Literaturzeitung.*

WA   *D. Martin Luthers Werke.* Kritische Gesamtausgabe.
        Weimar, 1930–   .
WA.BR   *D. Martin Luthers Werke.* Briefwechsel. Weimar,
        1930–   .
ZGW   *Zeitschrift für Geschichtswissenschaft.*
ZKG   *Zeitschrift für Kirchengeschichte.*

"In sum, I have done nothing but say that a Christian should not so wretchedly sacrifice someone else on the butcher's table. And if the political bigwigs do not cease to do so, the government should be taken from them. Whenever I have seriously proclaimed this to Christendom, it either refused to act or was too scared to do so. What more shall I do? Should I perhaps be silent, like a dumb dog? Why should I then make a living off the altar?"

Thomas Müntzer's farewell letter
to his Allstedt parish,
August 15, 1524. MSB 434:24—435:3.

PREFACE

Thomas Müntzer was the victim of a tragedy of errors, his own and those of his detractors. When he was executed as the perceived ideologist of the rebellious Saxon peasants on May 27, 1525, mainline Protestant reformers and defenders of Roman Catholicism appraised the event as God's just verdict on the man Luther had dubbed the "enthusiast" *(Schwärmer)* par excellence.

Müntzer lay buried in a tomb of sixteenth-century legend created by a hermeneutics of suspicion, until the nineteenth century. He was exhumed when historians discovered his literary remains, but there is still no consensus on the historical Müntzer. Primary sources have yielded just enough evidence to construct a biographical torso of the controversial reformer, which tempts scholars to speculate about the rest.

Two decades ago I produced a biographical study of Müntzer, based on research stimulated by my "doctor father," the late Roland H. Bainton.[1] Much Müntzeriana has been produced since then, and many detailed studies of aspects of Müntzer's life and work have appeared, including a massive "experiment in biography" by Walter Elliger.[2]

It may not be possible to produce the definitive biography of Müntzer because of a lack of sufficient evidence. But one can show how Müntzer developed his basic ideas and how he tried

1. Eric W. Gritsch, *Reformer Without a Church. The Life and Thought of Thomas Müntzer (1488?–1525)* (Philadelphia: Fortress Press, 1967).

2. Walter E. Elliger, *Thomas Müntzer. Leben und Werk* (Göttingen, W. Ger.: Vandenhoeck & Ruprecht, 1975).

to make them work for what he thought would be the last Christian reformation. Therefore, rather than revising my earlier work in a second edition, I offer now a summation of what I consider to be Müntzer's witness and legacy.

The book also commemorates Müntzer's five-hundredth birthday, even though the year of his birth cannot be established with absolute certainty. But there seems to be an emerging consensus that Müntzer could have been born in 1489. As a consequence, the German Democratic Republic has recommended a quincentenary celebration, to be held in 1989, to match, if not to exceed, that of Luther's quincentenary birthday celebrated in 1983.

Unless otherwise indicated, I have translated all non-English materials quoted in this book. I recommend Peter Matheson's translation of MSB, *The Collected Works of Thomas Müntzer.* I was unable to obtain this translation before my manuscript went to press. Müntzer specialists know how difficult it is to translate Müntzer, even into modern German. But Müntzer's rhetorical power and literary style deserve the closest possible hearing. Letting him speak to the reader, even in translation, may also provide greater historiographical clarity. The footnotes are limited to primary sources and to those secondary sources which assist the reader in understanding my own historical judgments concerning controversial data.

I am grateful to the administration and to the Board of Directors of the Lutheran Theological Seminary at Gettysburg for granting me a sabbatical leave in 1986 to do the necessary research and to begin the process of writing. I am grateful to Leif Grane and to Fortress Press, who have made helpful suggestions for the final version of this book. My spouse, Ruth, provided her usual, invaluable assistance as translator of German into English, as well as her expertise in editing and computerized word processing.

October 1988   ERIC W. GRITSCH

THOMAS MÜNTZER

1

THE QUEST FOR
AN INVINCIBLE FAITH

> I, Thomas Müntzer of Stolberg, confess before the entire church
> and the world . . . with Christ as my witness, and all the elect who
> have known me since childhood, that I have used the greatest
> diligence, more than anyone whom I have known, to receive a
> higher instruction in the holy, invincible Christian faith.

So wrote Müntzer on All Saints Day (November 1), 1521, from
Prague.[1] His early correspondence attests to his "diligence" in
searching for an invincible faith. But lack of solid historical
evidence leaves the historian in the dark about Müntzer's childhood and the formation of his early thought. There is no existing
record of anyone who might have known him well at that time.
Little can be told with certainty about Müntzer before 1517,
the year marked by the dissemination of Luther's Ninety-Five
Theses.

The year of Müntzer's birth can only be guessed at on the basis
of a prebend granted to him by St. Michael's Church in
Braunschweig on May 6, 1514. The document of presentation
calls Müntzer a "presbyter" *(presbiterus)*, a title applied to ordained priests, in the diocese of Halberstadt. *If* one assumes that
Müntzer was ordained shortly before he received the prebend,
and *if* at the time of his ordination he was twenty-five years old,
the minimum age required by Canon Law, then he could have
been born in 1489.[2]

---

1. Prague Manifesto, 1521. MSB 491:1–7.
2. The document of the prebend presentation is in MSB 553. The title "presbyter," ibid., 553:9. Most scholars agree that Müntzer may have been born

It may be assumed that Müntzer spent his childhood in Stolberg, a small town at the foot of the Harz Mountains, near the western border of what is now the German Democratic Republic (GDR). Müntzer's only mention of his parents is in a brief, scribbled note found in a book list. The note is addressed to his father, with whom he had quarrelled about a maternal dowry:

> I never expected to find you so disloyal . . . you deny me my natural rights, as if I were the child of a whore, or indeed a pagan. I am completely surprised that I should be expected to pay for your unconvincing opinion . . . that you were unable to support yourself. My mother brought plenty to you, as many people have testified to me in Stolberg and Quedlinburg. She earned her bread threefold.[3]

Stolberg had a solid Latin School where pupils could receive their elementary education beginning at the age of seven. They learned reading and writing in Latin, and received musical training such as singing in the local choir or learning to play an instrument.

Those who identify Thomas Müntzer as the "Müntzer of Quedlinburg" listed as a student in the Leipzig University records for 1506, surmise that his mother was from nearby Quedlinburg,[4] but the evidence is too circumstantial to warrant such a conclusion. Müntzer could have resided in Quedlinburg sometime before he began his university studies, because people there knew his parents. As such, he could be identified as a student at Leipzig University, which had been founded by German dissidents who had left the University of Prague in 1409. At the time Müntzer studied at Leipzig, a traditional curriculum prevailed. The Reformation and humanism had little, if any, effect on studies until the arrival in 1515 of the humanist Peter Moselanus, a supporter of Luther.

---

shortly before 1491. The data are well summarized and argued by Ulrich Bubenheimer, "Thomas Müntzer und der Anfang der Reformation in Braunschweig," *Nederlands Archief voor Kerksgeschedenis* 65 (1985): 5–6, 19. E, 27–28, suggests 1489, but links this hypothesis to other speculations regarding Müntzer's education for the priesthood and to family origins. See also chap. 9 below, pp. 123–125.

3. MSB 361:11–18.

4. See, for example, E, 11. But the evidence is too circumstantial to warrant such a conclusion.

A "Thomas Müntzer of Stolberg" first appears in the matriculation list of the University of Frankfurt an der Oder for the winter semester beginning on October 16, 1512. Someone later added "seditious" to his name to make it clear that this student was indeed the infamous radical of the Reformation.[5] The new university, founded in 1506 as the *Viadriana* in Frankfurt an der Oder, near what is now the eastern border of the GDR southeast of Berlin, was even less progressive than Leipzig. The curriculum stressed languages and law; and theologians there such as Conrad Wimpina, who served as president and dean, defended scholastic theology rather than humanism. Wimpina would later side with John Tetzel in the controversy with Luther regarding indulgences.

When interrogators asked him, under torture, whether he had been involved in other seditious activities besides the peasants' rebellion of 1525, Müntzer recalled only one event from his youth. The record states, "As a young assistant, he created a league in Aschersleben and Halle. . . . It was directed against the laudable memory of Bishop Ernest."[6] Ernest died in 1513. Müntzer could have spent some time in Halle and its vicinity, perhaps while visiting Leipzig and his friends nearby. There is evidence to show that some of the subjects of Ernest of Saxony, Archbishop of Magdeburg, criticized his rather worldly behavior, probably in some organized protest. Adherents to the Lutheran reform movement later (in the 1520s[7]) continued this kind of opposition to Albrecht, Archbishop of Magdeburg. Leipzig is only a short distance southeast of Halle and Aschersleben, so Müntzer could easily have travelled there.

---

5. Ernst Friedländer, ed., *Ältere Universitätsmatrikel. Universität Frankfurt an der Oder,* vol. 1, *1506–1648,* Publicationen aus den königlichen Preussischen Staatsarchiven 32 (Leipzig, 1887), 33–34.

6. Confession of May 16, 1525. MSB 548:28—549:3. This statement also names four co-conspirators from Aschersleben and Halle. "Assistant" *(collaborator)* may refer to a low position in the service of the church or in the school system. See E, 26.

7. It has been suggested that Müntzer admitted creating an organized protest in Halle before 1513 in order to cover up his involvement in similar activities in Halle sometime between 1521 and 1523. See Otto Schiff, "Thomas Müntzer als Prediger in Halle," ARG 23 (1926): 287–93, esp. 292–93. But if Müntzer was really born shortly before 1491, any such involvement as a "young assistant" is more plausible around 1512 rather than after 1521. See also E, 29–32.

4 THOMAS MÜNTZER: A TRAGEDY OF ERRORS

Müntzer eventually received the degrees of Bachelor of Arts, Master of Arts, and the Biblical Baccalaureate, but no records exist which show the institutions from which he earned these degrees.[8] He was probably ordained shortly before receiving a prebend from St. Michael's in Braunschweig on May 6, 1514, and he may have served as a priest there. Early correspondence also reveals that Müntzer served as a chaplain to nuns at a convent in Frohse, near Halle, which was specifically a "foundation for canonesses" *(Kanonissenstift)* who lived under a rule rather than taking vows. This foundation was a branch of a larger foundation in Gernrode, headed by the abbess Elizabeth von Weida. But what Müntzer's duties were can only be surmised based on his title *praepositus*.[9] He obviously celebrated masses and heard confessions.

Ludolf Witthovet, a fellow prebendary in Braunschweig, wrote to Müntzer in Frohse complaining about Müntzer's rela-

8. Müntzer usually referred to himself, or was addressed by others, as "Master of Arts and Baccalaureus (Bachelor) of Holy Scripture" *(artium magister et sancte scripture baccalaureus)*, MSB 537:14. He was addressed as such in 1517–18 (MSB 347:11) and in 1521 (MSB 373:12–13). What he may have studied at Frankfurt an der Oder can only be surmised. See Günter Vogler, "Thomas Müntzer als Student der Viadriana" in *Die Oder-Universität Frankfurt. Beiträge zu ihrer Geschichte* (Weimar: Böhlaus Nachfolger, 1983), 243–51. Modern biographers concede that Müntzer may have resided in Quedlinburg before he matriculated at Leipzig University in 1506. See E, 11. Manfred Bensing, *Thomas Müntzer*, 3d ed., rev. (Leipzig: VEB Bibliographisches Institut, 1983), 16–17. Siegfried Bräuer and Hans Jürgen Goertz, "Thomas Müntzer" in *Gestalten der Kirchengeschichte*, vol. 5, *Die Reformationszeit I*, ed. Martin Greschat (Stuttgart, Köln, Mainz: Kohlhammer, 1981), 335. Bubenheimer ("Thomas Müntzer und der Anfäng," 21, n. 104) contends that "there is no compelling argument" *(kein zwingendes Argument)* for a thesis claiming Müntzer studied at Leipzig, because there is no solid evidence that Müntzer resided in Quedlinburg. But Bubenheimer later regarded the study at Leipzig as "probable" *(wahrscheinlich)*. See Bubenheimer, "Thomas Müntzer's Wittenberger Studienzeit," ZKG 99 (1988): 169. Müntzer himself linked his parents to Quedlinburg (MSB 361:16–18). Attempts have been made to reconstruct Müntzer's educational experiences on the basis of what is generally known about medieval schools and universities. See, for example, the reconstruction in E, 18–25, 32–38. But it is not even certain that Müntzer studied theology at a university (ibid., 38).

9. The title does not appear in Frohse, but tradition associates it with chaplains to nuns. See Philipp Hofmeister, "Propst" in *Lexikon für Theologie und Kirche*, 10 vols., 2d ed., rev. (Freiburg: Herder, 1963), 8:809. A newly edited letter to Müntzer from August 1516 calls him "pastor in Frohse." See the edition of Bubenheimer (based on MSB 347) in "Thomas Müntzer in Braunschweig," Part 1, *Braunschweiger Jahrbuch* 65 (1984):55, 70, 2.3. Müntzer could have resided in the Frohse parsonage. What is known has been summarized in E, 40, but no significant conclusions are offered.

tions with women and particularly with his cook; he accused the cook of having spread rumors about him, thus driving him to vacate a room that could be heated in winter. He also referred to a quarrel between himself and Müntzer, giving rise to the speculation that they had shared rooms in Braunschweig.[10] A well-to-do citizen of Aschersleben, Matthew Volmar, wrote to Müntzer in Frohse on August 30, 1516, expressing his appreciation for some medical advice concerning a throat ailment.[11]

Sometime before July 1517, the rector of the School of St. Martin in Braunschweig wrote to Müntzer in Frohse to ask the "learned man" (virus perdoctus) the following questions: How does one define the relationship between sinful human nature and divine forgiveness? What is the meaning of indulgences? How are such questions related to the authority of the pope? How are they related to the distinction between priesthood and laity?[12] Unfortunately, any answers from Müntzer have been lost. Another letter, written between 1515 and July 25, 1517, addressed Müntzer as "persecutor of injustice," a hint that he played a particular role in Braunschweig.[13]

This correspondence, as well as contacts between Müntzer and other people in Braunschweig, point to Müntzer's possible involvement in a controversy over indulgences there, perhaps in

10. Undated letter. MSB 350. Bubenheimer ("Thomas Müntzer in Braunschweig," Part 1, 69, 2.2) reedited this letter and dates it tentatively at 1515–16. The text does not disclose the exact circumstances of Müntzer's relationship with Witthovet or with the cook. Bubenheimer surmises (op. cit., 54) that either Müntzer and Witthovet lived together in Braunschweig, or that Müntzer commuted between Braunschweig and Frohse. Such a conclusion is questionable, but Bubenheimer's careful analysis of all of Müntzer's contacts in and around Braunschweig points to his having known a variety of people involved in various trades. Bubenheimer calls this Müntzer's "social interlacing" (soziale Verflechtungen), op. cit. Part 2, 79.

11. MSB 347 no. 1.

12. MSB 347—48. Newly edited by Bubenheimer, "Thomas Müntzer in Braunschweig," Part 1, 70, 2.4.

13. Claus, servant of Hans Pelt, to Müntzer on July 25, 1517. MSB 349:4. Newly edited by Bubenheimer, "Thomas Müntzer in Braunschweig," Part 1, 67–68, 2.1. The origin of the phrase "persecutor of injustice" (vorfolger der unrechtverdicheyt) is unclear. It is doubtful that it refers to Müntzer's activities in Braunschweig. See Siegfried Bräuer, "Thomas Müntzers Beziehungen zur Braunschweiger Frühreformation," Theologische Literaturzeitung 109 (1984): 636–38. Bubenheimer (op. cit., 28) thinks the term has mystical origins but cannot provide proof. E, 44 relates it to Müntzer's earlier involvement in controversy in Aschersleben and Halle. See above, p. 3.

the summer of 1517. There is some evidence indicating that John Tetzel, the infamous preacher of indulgences, was in Braunschweig in the summer of 1517. The bull of Pope Leo X, issued on March 31, 1515, in response to a request from Archbishop Albrecht of Mainz, had permitted the sale of indulgences. On the feast of St. Peter and St. Paul, June 29, 1517, a Benedictine monastery in Königslutter near Braunschweig attracted many pilgrims to the proclamation of indulgences. In such a context Müntzer could have joined in criticizing indulgences, indeed in opposing them. The rector of St. Martin in Braunschweig was a well-educated man who studied in Wittenberg in 1518 and seems to have shared the critical stance of many intellectuals toward Rome.[14]

The only surviving writings of Müntzer from the Frohse period are copies he made of liturgical texts: two Offices of St. Cyriacus and one Hallelujah to St. Cyriacus, whose martyrdom at the hands of the Romans had been commemorated on August 8 since 354 C.E. These texts had been used in various missals in German,[15] and Müntzer seemingly penned them from memory, which discloses his early interest in liturgy. Müntzer's heading on these copies was the puzzling statement, "That I may not be deceived by error" *(ne errore decipia)*, which could be interpreted either as a heartfelt ejaculation *(Stossseufzer)* commonly used at that time or as a sign of his spiritual anxiety. But in view of the very limited evidence, it is not really possible to state whether Müntzer experienced any kind of spiritual anxiety in Frohse.[16]

14. Bubenheimer has argued passionately for Müntzer's link to a possible indulgences controversy in Braunschweig; a summary appears in "Thomas Müntzer und der Anfang," esp. 9–18, 22–29. Bensing (*Thomas Müntzer*, 25) thinks that Müntzer taught at the school of St. Martin, but there is no solid evidence for such a conclusion. Müntzer may have taught sons of Halberstadt friends, since he received money for such services while in Frohse. July 25, 1517, letter from Claus. MSB 349:6–12, 18.

15. Analysis and edition of the texts by Friedrich Wiechert in MSB 481—90.

16. Quoted in MSB 485:1. Wiechert (MSB 484) produced evidence for such *Stossseufzer* in the medieval liturgical tradition. "Müntzer asks God in this 'heading' to assist him in his copying and to keep him from making mistakes." E, 42–43, tries to link the expression to a feeling of disappointment produced by the tension between pious liturgical externals and Müntzer's drive for "a higher instruction," as was expressed in the Prague Manifesto of 1521. See above, n. 1. Others surmise that the heading expresses "a certain inner restlessness." See Annemarie Lohmann, *Zur geistigen Entwicklung Thomas Müntzers*, Beiträge zur Kulturgeschichte des Mittelalters und der Renaissance 47 (Leipzig and Berlin: Teubner, 1931), 5.

The fragmentary evidence that does exist for the period between 1489 and 1517 suggests that Müntzer spent his childhood in a small town, attended a good elementary school in Stolberg, and, as a university student, pursued his early quest for the origins of the true Christian faith. His studies led him to ordination into the priesthood. He had no difficulties attaining the regular graduate degrees, and he soon became known as a learned priest committed to teaching and to critical discernment of the climate of opinion on the eve of the Reformation. His contacts in Braunschweig, located a short distance north of Stolberg, provided the young priest with an income and involved him in altercations about the significance of indulgences, which was the subject of critical debate between churchmen and theologians and which concerned political leaders who sought ecclesiastical reform.

On October 31, 1517, Luther posted his Ninety-five Theses, calling for clarification on the use of indulgences. In another set of theses, Luther defended St. Augustine's views on sin and grace and opposed Aristotle's influence on medieval scholastic theology.[17] Many priests, theologians, and lay people supported him, including a Wittenberg student named Franz Günther. Günther had been a student in 1514 when Luther lectured on Psalms and suggested new theological directions to follow. Günther earned his degree of Bachelor of Holy Scripture on September 4, 1517, by successfully defending Luther's *Disputation Against Scholastic Theology* according to the custom of the time, which was that students defended the work of their teacher in public debate before receiving their academic degrees.

As Luther's reform movement grew and necessitated local leadership, Jüterbog, a town northeast of Wittenberg, called for Günther as a "Lutheran" pastor. Upon his arrival in January 1519, he immediately became embroiled in controversy with the Catholic establishment, especially with the Franciscans. The Jüterbog Franciscan friar Bernard Dappen sent a detailed report of this controversy to the Bishop of Brandenburg, Jerome Schulz, who was also Luther's superior. The report summarizes

17. *Disputation Against Scholastic Theology*, 1517. WA 1:221–28. LW 31:9–16.

Günther's preaching "after the period of Lent" in the form of four theses:

1. one need not go to confession because there is no such commandment in Scripture.
2. one need not fast, because Christ had fasted for us.
3. one need not invoke the saints.
4. the Bohemians [Hussites] are better Christians than "we."[18]

According to Dappen, there had been a debate between the Franciscans and the "sectarians" led by Günther who had contended, among other things, that neither pope nor ecclesiastical councils represented the universal church, and who had obviously defended Luther's views. But, Dappen added, when the bishop reprimanded Günther, who had visited him regarding these matters, Günther refrained from preaching for some time. Dappen continued:

> At that time [around Easter 1519] another *magister* of the same sect arrived. His name was Thomas and he had shortly before been driven from Braunschweig. He [Günther] let him preach for a while as his substitute—I know not by whose permission—probably with the intention of having someone else accomplish, without fear of accountability, what he himself did not dare to do out of fear of the gracious Bishop of Brandenburg.[19]

In a personal letter accompanying the official report to the bishop, Dappen stated that Günther "had called in a Magister Thomas from Wittenberg."[20] Since there is no reason to doubt the veracity of this report, Müntzer must have left Frohse sometime in the summer of 1517 and gone to Jüterbog in the spring of 1519. He could have traveled from Braunschweig to Wittenberg, perhaps with Heinrich Hanner, his Braunschweig friend who had been the head of the School of St. Martin and matriculated at the University of Wittenberg on June 3, 1518.[21] He may have

18. Manfred Bensing and Winfried Trillitzsch, "Bernhard Dappens 'Articuli ... contra Lutheranos.' Zur Auseinandersetzung der Jüterboger Franziskaner mit Thomas Müntzer und Franz Günther 1519," ZGW 14 (1967): 113–47, citation 133. Latin text with German translation.

19. Ibid., 137.

20. Ibid., 143.

21. See a summary of his career in Bubenheimer, "Thomas Müntzer und der Anfang," 17–18.

been "driven from Braunschweig," as Dappen put it, because of his opposition to the abuse of indulgences. In any case, Müntzer spent an extended period of time in Wittenberg, probably from October 1517 to April 1519.[22] He could have been visiting his friend Günther and another friend, the goldsmith Christian Döring; and he could have observed Luther's first moves against Catholic abuses. No doubt Müntzer was attracted to Luther and his movement. At any rate, they met sometime between 1517 and 1518, although little, if anything, is known about any meetings. Luther later said that "he [Müntzer] has been in my cloister in Wittenberg once or twice and had his nose punched."[23]

During the winter semester of 1517–18 Müntzer attended lectures on St. Jerome (340/50–420), the famous church father who produced the Latin Bible (Vulgate), exemplary biblical commentaries, homilies, historical works, and an extensive correspondence about ecclesiastical affairs. The lectures were probably given by John Rhagius Aesticampianus, a young instructor and humanist eager to initiate students into the philosophy of classical antiquity as an alternative to scholasticism. He was an itinerant teacher, and the administration of the University of Wittenberg had persuaded him to offer courses in philosophy and theology. He used his humanistic skills in interpreting texts to lecture on St. Jerome. According to newly discovered fragmentary notes in his handwriting, Müntzer attended Rhagius's lectures with the intention to pursue humanistic studies.[24] He seemed to be impressed by Plato as a role model for philosophers, by the notion that much is learned through travel, and by the relationship of learning to suffering.[25]

22. See Bubenheimer, "Thomas Müntzers Wittenberger Studienzeit," 176–77. His argument is based on new evidence. Bensing (*Thomas Müntzer*, 27) also opts for a stay in 1517. E 51 surmises that Müntzer went to Wittenberg in November 1518, after a stopover with friends in Halberstadt and Aschersleben.

23. *Letter to the Princes of Saxony Concerning the Rebellious Spirit*, 1524. WA 15:214.4–5, LW 40:52. See also Müntzer's *Highly Necessary Defense and Answer Against the Soft-Living Flesh of Wittenberg . . .*, 1524, MSB 341:10–11: "I have not been with you in six or seven years."

24. These fragments have been unearthed by Ulrich Bubenheimer and published in "Thomas Müntzers Nachschrift einer Wittenberger Hieronymusvorlesung," ZKG 99 (1988): 228–37. The St. Jerome text is a letter to the presbyter Paul *(Epistula 53 ad Paulinum)*, according to a 1517 edition.

25. See Bubenheimer, "Thomas Müntzers Wittenberger Studienzeit," 189–92.

Whether Müntzer stayed in Wittenberg or travelled elsewhere during this period is uncertain. There is evidence to show that he spent some time in Leipzig, since Döring wrote to him there. In the letter, Döring, who was an influential citizen in Wittenberg, informed Müntzer that he had recommended him for the post of assistant pastor *(kaplan)* in nearby Feldkirch under the tutelage of the Lutheran provost Bartholomy Bernardi.[26] But Müntzer obviously preferred to go to Jüterbog.

Müntzer's preaching in Jüterbog at the Church of the Virgin Mary identified him clearly as a "Martinian," an adherent of the new reform movement. On Easter Sunday (April 24, 1519), he preached against the Franciscans, accusing them of ignorance, of not even knowing that the Bible had been written in Hebrew and Greek. Perhaps the city council had hired him; certainly he had the encouragement of a majority of Jüterbog citizens for his attacks. On Easter Monday he preached another sermon which Dappen considered heretical. When Dappen tried to inform a crowd of people of Müntzer's "heresy," Müntzer responded with another sermon on April 26.

Dappen reported to Bishop Schulz the statements in Müntzer's sermons which he considered most offensive: that the pope should convene a council every five years instead of only three times in four hundred years; that councils could assemble without the will of the pope; that the pope should keep his authority only as long as bishops granted it; that the canonization of saints was the business of councils, and the pope had no right to canonize anyone, as he had done with St. Bonaventure and St. Thomas; that these and other scholastic teachers based their theology on reason, but that an argument based on reason is of the devil; that bishops should visit their subjects every year and examine their faith, just as school principals do; that this would eliminate the fear of "bats and moles" (Isa. 2:20), of citations and excommunications, which are all devilish things; that

Whether these fragmentary texts reveal the roots of Müntzer's later views, e.g., his "theology of suffering" *(Leidenstheologie)* is questionable (ibid., 191). But Bubenheimer's basic conclusion is convincing: Müntzer encountered not only Luther but also a humanism that had an enduring effect on his life and thought (ibid., 192).

26. Letter dated January 11, 1519. MSB 351.

the rule of bishops was a rule of tyrants rather than of bishops in the church, and if priests were to complain they would now be arrested rather than, as in the past, simply removed from office; that the gospel had been pushed into the corner during the last four hundred years, and people now had to risk their lives to bring it back into prominence.

Dappen then reminded the bishop that Müntzer and Günther shared the intention of such heretics as the fourth-century Donatists, who also had refused to accept the sacraments from bishops and then betrayed their faith when persecuted. He added that they, like all schismatics, tear apart the seamless coat of Christ (John 19:23–24) and threaten the unity of the church with their senseless attacks on monks. The bishop must move against them, he pleaded, especially since they were leading common people into error, like snakes in the grass—even though it might take fifty years to overcome them.[27]

When Bishop Schulz received this report, he asked John Eck to draw up a theological "opinion" *(Gutachten)* about the controversy. Eck, who was eager to refute Luther's theology, quickly penned a statement identifying sixteen heretical Lutheran items. Luther reacted as soon as he read Eck's and Dappen's attacks. First he reprinted Eck's hasty "opinion," charging him with twenty-four counts of false teaching. Then he wrote a nasty letter to the Franciscans in Jüterbog. He declared that what Günther and Müntzer had preached corresponded to the gospel and was by no means "pernicious error." Regarding Müntzer, he stated:

> I do not know what Thomas has preached, I only see again how your own evil betrays itself. For when he plucks the prelates, popes and bishops in general—something that not only is permitted but must happen (unless you deny Scripture and want to hinder it) since in it Christ deals very hard with thieves, robbers, and wolves—you dare to make it his fault. You would have been right if he had mentioned any person by name. But now you are the slanderers and deceitful accusers, because you do not understand him correctly. Whatever you take up, you do so in the way you understand it and then speak about it carelessly. When will you

27. Bensing and Trillitzsch, op. cit., 139–41.

render satisfaction *to him and to us (illi et nobis)* for such heavy offence?[28]

In the spring of 1519, therefore, Luther clearly regarded Müntzer as a supporter of his reform movement and defended him as such. Even though Dappen's report about Müntzer's preaching must be read with caution, in view of its polemical context, there is no doubt that Müntzer was perceived as a member of the new Wittenberg "sect," as Dappen put it. Müntzer's Jüterbog message that pope and council could no longer be trusted anticipated by a few months Luther's contention at the Leipzig debate that the pope had no absolute authority over against councils and Scripture, and so he, like Müntzer, was called a Hussite.[29]

There is some evidence to show that Müntzer was in Leipzig during the famous Leipzig debate between Andreas Bodenstein of Carlstadt (known as Carlstadt) and John Eck from June 27 to July 3 and between Luther and Eck from July 4 to 14, 1519. In a letter to the Leipzig accountant Achatius Glor, dated January 3, 1520, Müntzer noted that he had bought books "at the time of the disputation" *(disputationis tempore).*[30] There is also a lengthy note from one of Müntzer's acquaintances in Orlamünde, Konrad Glitzsch, who asked Müntzer to buy a variety of items in Leipzig, including groceries, tools, and books; he mentioned Carlstadt and asked Müntzer to deliver greetings to Luther and other Wittenbergers.[31] Glitzsch was the vicar of the Orlamünde parish, southwest of Leipzig. This parish was a part of the All Saints Foundation *(Allerheiligenstift),* reserved for the arch-

28. Luther's letter of May 15, 1519. WA. BR 1:392. 107–15. Italics mine. See also his response to Eck in WA 2:625–54.

29. Luther's statement at Leipzig is summarized in thesis 13, which denies the absolute superiority of the papacy over against councils and Scripture. WA 2:161.35–38. LW 31:318. See also the detailed defense of thesis 13 in WA 2:180–240. Bensing *(Thomas Müntzer,* 29–30) contends that Müntzer went beyond Luther in his statements in Jüterbog; that he attacked the tyranny and ignorance of bishops; and that he denied the authority of councils because they no longer call the pope and the bishops into account. Accordingly, Bensing declared, Müntzer was not Luther's "disciple" *(Schüler)* but an "ally" *(Bundesgenosse).* But this distinction is hard to prove. E, 65 calls Müntzer more appropriately "an advocate of the Reformation concern" *(Verfechter des reformatorischen Anliegens).*

30. MSB 353:23—354:1.

31. MSB 554—55.

deacon who was a professor at the university. In 1519 it happened to be Carlstadt, Luther's Wittenberg colleague and dean of the university. A careful analysis of the text and context of the notes suggests that Glitzsch wrote it in 1519 (perhaps in February) and that Müntzer may have spent some time in Orlamünde (perhaps two or three months before he appeared in Jüterbog on April 24, 1519).[32]

That Müntzer may have resided at Orlamünde is also attested by Pastor Martin Glaser, one of Carlstadt's successors in Orlamünde. Glaser wrote a marginal note in an edition of sermons by the German Dominican mystic John Tauler (ca. 1300–61), which Luther had given him in 1519. It said:

> Thomas Müntzer and his adherents have been seduced by Tauler's teaching on the Spirit and the depth of the soul *(Grund der Seele)*, which they do not understand. He [Müntzer] always read him (as we well know and as is well known) in the company of a woman who had been Master Conrad's [Glitzsch] cook, and who carried on in such a peculiar way so that she was regarded as a saint. Müntzer learned quite a few of his errors from her. Andreas Carlstadt followed him in believing such errors and was also seduced. They hatched and disseminated their errors in Orlamünde.... I knew both well.[33]

In his search for historical and psychological religious certainty, Müntzer could easily have been drawn to Tauler. Luther too had spoken very highly of the German mystics, especially Tauler, in 1516; he edited the *Theologica Germanica* in 1518, suggesting Tauler as the author. "Next to the Bible and St. Augustine," he declared in the introduction, "no other book has come to my attention from which I have learned—and desired to learn—more concerning God, Christ, man, and what all things are."[34]

It is not known whether Müntzer and Luther met in Leipzig,

32. These are the convincing conclusions of Bubenheimer, "Thomas Müntzers Wittenberger Studienzeit," 201–202.

33. Quoted in E, 66–67, and in Bubenheimer, "Thomas Müntzers Wittenberger Studienzeit," 202–203. Bubenheimer shows why Kaspar Glatz was confused with Martin Glaser (ibid., 203, n. 233).

34. See *The Theologica Germanica of Martin Luther.* Translation, Introduction, and Commentary by Bengt Hoffman, The Classics of Western Spirituality (New York: Ramsey; Toronto: Paulist Press, 1980), 54.

but much later (1524), when Müntzer denounced Luther as a
satanic opponent of the true reformation which he, Müntzer,
represented, he disclosed a detailed knowledge of the Leipzig
debate. "You felt very contented," he told Luther, "leaving the
city with a wreath of carnations and drinking good wine at
Melchior Lotter's house."[35] Müntzer probably knew that detail
from Lotter, since he bought several books from the famous
printer.[36]

Sometime before or in December 1519, Müntzer accepted the
position of father confessor at the Cistercian nunnery at Beuditz,
near Weissenfels, southwest of Leipzig. Linked historically to
the mystical tradition of St. Bernard of Clairvaux (1090–1153),
the nunnery was located in a peaceful setting quite removed
from the turbulence caused by Luther's conflict with Rome.
Müntzer hinted at a reason for going there in a letter to his
friend Franz Günther, dated January 1, 1520:[37] he went because
he needed an income and a place to stay. He told Günther that he
was compelled to go to Beuditz, but did not mind being there
since he had few liturgical duties and could use his time to
reread St. Augustine and other historical works. He admitted
that he had difficulties understanding most of the authors he
was reading, but added that he was nevertheless content with
his state of mind, because not he, Müntzer, but Jesus was the
best judge in such matters. The letter ends with the admission
that he felt himself to be judged by God because he often
preached without inner compulsion, a fact that made him feel
miserable. "I have nothing but your love, which I shall inhibit
with my loquacity."

Two days later, Müntzer wrote to Achatius Glor, Lotter's em-
ployee in Leipzig, listing books he had received and books he
still needed. Among them were the church history by Eusebius
of Caesarea, which depicted the rise of Christianity from its
beginning to its acceptance under Constantine the Great in

35. *Highly Necessary Defense* . . . , MSB 340:22–24. The "wreath of carnations"
was actually a bouquet Luther carried with him. Legend transformed it into a
wreath on his head.

36. See the substantial bill and letter from Achatius Glor, one of Lotter's em-
ployees, dated January 3, 1520, MSB 355. The bill supports the contention, E, 68,
that Müntzer was a "bibliomaniac" *(Büchernarr)*.

37. MSB 352—53. Quotation, 353:12–13.

324 C.E.; Flavius Josephus's history of the Jewish war against the Romans ending with the fall of Massada in 73 C.E.; Jerome Emser's polemical treatise against Luther, entitled *Assertion of the Leipzig Goat Against Luther's Hunt*, 1519; a concordance of Canon Law; the newly edited (1518) continuation of Eusebius's church history by Jerome; the complete works of Jerome (345–420), edited in nine volumes by Erasmus in 1516–18; the 1516–17 Paris editions of the letters and sermons of Augustine (354–430); the acts of the general councils of Constance (1414–18) and Basel (1431–49).[38] By the end of 1520, Müntzer had made a list of seventy-four book titles, seemingly intending either to buy them or to pay for them. These titles mainly represent works published in 1519 and 1520, and include writings by Luther, Carlstadt, and several humanists.[39]

Sometime after Müntzer left Beuditz, perhaps in May of 1520, a nun named Ursula sent him some homemade bread and, in the context of fond memories of her father confessor, made some cryptic remarks referring to his study of the German mystics Tauler and Henry Suso: "I don't care if either Tauler or Brother Suso taught you, or if you read in their writings that you should buy gifts for beautiful maidens during the annual church fair."[40] Müntzer had obviously used his time in Beuditz to study Christian origins and to keep in touch with developments linked to Luther's reform movement. He had also kept in touch with friends and acquaintances, some of whom criticized him for becoming involved in the affairs of others without knowing all the details, and for making hasty and indiscriminate judgments.[41]

Much of what had seemed so secure in the medieval tradition was now being questioned. Luther and humanists such as Erasmus of Rotterdam had begun an investigation, based on critical editions of the sources, of the origins of the Christian church.

38.. MSB 353—54.

39. MSB 556—60. The editor speculates that Müntzer might have received the list from someone at the Leipzig Book Fair in the fall of 1520, or that he might even have ordered these books because of a special Fair discount.

40. MSB 356. Quotation: 356:16–18.

41. See, for example, the letter dated December 12, 1519, from John of Weida, a Leipzig Dominican, who criticized this trait. MSB 351:13–16.

The Leipzig debate had focused on the question of ecclesiastical authority: Did papal authority exist from the very beginning of Christianity? Could pope and councils err? Müntzer felt himself to be a part of this quest for historical truth, and so became a bookworm in a nunnery.

Müntzer's study of Christian origins and of theologians like Augustine and Tauler may have provided some answers to his quest for an invincible faith. All of his free time was devoted to the exploration of the past as well as the present. In the earliest accounts of Christian history, he could read how Christians had suffered and died for their faith; and how under Constantine the Great the sudden adoption of Christianity had created a superficial and bureaucratic church based on the casuistry of an ever-expanding Canon Law. It was perhaps Augustine, Luther's favorite church father, who taught Müntzer the pessimistic view of an earthly life plagued by struggle between sin and grace, and the imminence of the end of the world when Christ would come again to establish his rule forever. Jerome, on the other hand, was known for the ascetic discipline he employed in consistent defense of the church, the guardian of Scripture; the *Vulgate*, the church-approved Latin version of Scripture was Jerome's creation.

Reading the acts of the ecclesiastical councils of Constance and Basel certainly revealed to Müntzer the papal schisms that plagued Europe from 1309 to 1377, the period known as the "Babylonian captivity of the papacy" in which one pope ruled in Avignon and another in Rome. He also learned from these councils of the struggle between the Curialists, who defended papal authority, and the Conciliarists, who advocated the council's authority over the pope.

Since Müntzer, like Luther, was dubbed a Hussite, he undoubtedly read the account of John Hus's martyrdom at Constance in 1415—the event that triggered the fierce Hussite wars between the emperor and Hus adherents in Bohemia and Moravia. But Müntzer studied the mystical ideas of Tauler and Suso above all others, for they dealt largely with the soul's doubt and despair before the "birth of God" within it. Tauler was known for his allegorical interpretation of Scripture in sermons filled with admonitions that one must overcome the flesh by attaining complete independence from creatureliness in a kind of "yieldedness" *(Gelassenheit)*.[42] Müntzer could have encountered in the *Theologica Germanica* (attributed to Tauler by Luther) the belief that one can reach God only through God rather than through the use of human reason, and that this causes inner suffering.

All these sources could have struck a responsive chord in the mind of the father confessor charged with providing the comfort of divine forgiveness for the nuns at Beuditz. The language of the German mystics, especially Tauler, Suso, and Master Eckhart (ca. 1260–1328) certainly played a significant role in his development.[43]

But Müntzer's search for historical truth and exploration of the self at Beuditz soon came to an end. On April 21, 1520, the archdeacon of Elsterberg wrote him a letter from Leipzig asking him to consider a position as vicar *(conventor)*.[44] Müntzer must have declined the offer, because he accepted a position as substitute priest for the vacationing John Egranus, pastor at St. Mary's in Zwickau. He delivered his first sermon, either on Rogation Sunday (May 13, 1521) or on Ascension Day (May 17).[45] Luther had recommended him for the position, telling the arch-

42. So translated in George H. Williams and Angel M. Mergal, eds., *Spiritual and Anabaptist Writers*, vol. 25 of The Library of Christian Classics (Philadelphia: Westminster Press, 1957), 272. The term *Gelassenheit* was widely used by mystical and other writers in the sixteenth century. See the examples cited by E. Gordon Rupp, *Patterns of Reformation* (Philadelphia: Fortress Press, 1969), 118, n. 4.

43. That Müntzer's theology derived from, or originated in "the gradient of medieval mysticism" *(Traditionsgefälle der mittelalterlichen Mystik)* has been forcefully argued by Hans-Jürgen Goertz, *Innere und äussere Ordnung in der Theologie Thomas Müntzers*, Studies in the History of Christian Thought 2, ed. Heiko A. Oberman (Leiden, Neth.: E. J. Brill, 1967), esp. chap. 2. A similar interpretation was offered earlier, in conjunction with Müntzer's dependence on "medieval sects" in general and on Joachim of Fiore in particular. See M. M. Smirin, *Die Volksreformation des Thomas Müntzer und der grosse Bauernkrieg*, trans. from Russian by Hans Nichtweiss, 2d. ed., rev. (Berlin: Dietz, 1952), esp. chaps. 2—4. But Müntzer was not the systematic thinker portrayed by Goertz, even though German medieval mysticism played a decisive role in his theological reflections. Goertz later modified his position in "Der Mystiker mit dem Hammer," KD 20 (1974): 23–53. At this time he mentioned other "apercus" *(Gedankensplitter)* as well as mystical reflections. See ibid., 31. For a critical appreciation of Goertz in the context of an analysis of Müntzer's concept of faith, see Eric W. Gritsch, "Müntzers Glaubensverständnis" in *Der Theologe und Thomas Müntzer*, ed. Siegfried Bräuer and Helmar Junghans (Berlin: Evangelische Verlagsanstalt; Göttingen: Van den Hoeck & Ruprecht, 1989).

44. MSB 355—56, esp. 356:2.

45. It is difficult to decide which of the two sources for these dates is more reliable. See E, 77.

deacon Henry of Buenau that "Thomas Müntzer could not be moved from his purpose" of going to Zwickau. "Yet I am glad," he added, "that all the vicars and chaplains have become attentive to the work of grace."[46] It is thus evident that Müntzer was at this time considered a reliable candidate for a ministry dedicated to Luther's reform movement.

46. WA.BR 2:109.3–4. English translation in LC 1:324. Egranus, in a letter to Luther dated May 18, 1521, attests to the fact that Luther recommended Müntzer for the position in Zwickau. WA.BR 2:346, n.a.: ". . . whom you had recommended to me at Leipzig."

2

TESTING THE WATERS
OF THE REFORMATION

Zwickau, known as "the pearl of Saxony,[1]" was an important Saxon city between the Thuringian basin and the Bohemian foothills in what is now the southern part of the GDR. One of Europe's major trade routes ran through Zwickau, it linked the ports of the Hanseatic League in the north with Prague and other trade centers in the east. Weaver guilds produced textiles, and the silver mines in the nearby hills attracted a lot of business. The two largest churches in town were St. Mary's and St. Catherine's, and the most visible monastic community was the Franciscan order. The Franciscans clung to Roman Catholicism even though the city fathers and most of the townspeople had switched to Luther's reform movement.

George Agricola, a pioneer in scientific mineralogy who was also versed in philosophy and theology, was headmaster of the local school, where students learned Latin and Greek and were trained in the humanistic liberal arts. Humanism advocated reform through an education grounded in faithfulness to the roots of Western culture, to the philosophical traditions of ancient Greece and Rome, and to the teachings of Holy Scripture. By 1520, many humanists supported Luther's movement, al-

---

1. For a sketch of local history, see Paul Wappler, *Thomas Müntzer in Zwickau und die "Zwickauer Propheten,"* Schriften des Vereins für Reformationsgeschichte 182, 2d ed., rev. (Gütersloh, W. Ger.: Gerd Mohn, 1966), 7–20. A more accurate account of the religious situation, especially the beginnings of the Reformation in Zwickau, is offered by Anne-Rose Fröhlich, "Die Einführung der Reformation in Zwickau," *Mitteilungen des Altertumsvereins für Zwickau und Umgebung* 12 (1919): 1–74.

though Luther would soon separate himself from Erasmus and Erasmian ideas.[2] Elector Frederick "the Wise" did not oppose the young professor teaching in Wittenberg; nor did he condemn the burgeoning ecclesiastical reform in Zwickau. But in the spring of 1520, no one could yet judge with certainty how the Wittenberg movement would succeed over against Rome.

John Sylvius Egranus (whose real name was Wildenhauer but who used the Latinized version of Eger, his hometown) was the leading clergyman in Zwickau.[3] Like many other learned priests, Egranus found intellectual comfort in humanism. Egranus became involved in difficulties with the local Franciscans when he criticized the cult of St. Anne, the favorite saint of the miners and the alleged mother of the Virgin Mary. However, the bishop of the diocese of Naumburg chose to tolerate the Zwickau developments, especially after Egranus sent him a sophisticated defense of his position concerning the cult of St. Anne.[4]

At the time Egranus was granted one of his frequent leaves of absence to pursue academic studies, this controversy was still in the air. The city fathers of Zwickau revealed their preference for Luther and his movement when they chose Müntzer to become temporary pastor of St. Mary's during Egranus's absence. Müntzer immmediately attacked the Franciscans from the pulpit, just as he had done in Jüterbog: "The monks have such big mouths that, even if one pound were cut off, they'd still have enough left to continue with their prattling."[5]

On July 13, 1520, Müntzer sent Luther an account of his initial experiences at St. Mary's, explaining that he was advised to do so by the city council, which desired Luther's counsel on the controversy. Citing a number of biblical passages from memory and using pompous rhetoric, Müntzer described his encounter

2. After the literary debate on the bondage and freedom of human will in 1525. See WA 18:600–787; LW 33.

3. Hubert Kirchner wrote an intellectual biography, *Johannes Sylvius Egranus. Ein Beitrag zum Verhältnis von Reformation und Humanismus*, Aufsätze und Vorträge zur Theologie und Religionswissenschaft 21 (Berlin: Evangelische Verlagsanstalt, 1961).

4. Egranus questioned the tradition that claimed Anne had three husbands. Details in Kirchner, *Johann Sylvius Egranus*, 32–36.

5. According to a report by the Zwickauer Peter Schulmann. Quoted in E, 78.

with the "hypocrites," whom he had exposed as "monsters" who claimed they wore the helmet and shield of faith (Eph. 6:16) but who in reality were noisy ceremonialists raging before the people and accusing him of destroying Christian love.[6] He, on the contrary, was really the faithful adherent to the Word of God, whose instrument he was.

> I take in all the false absurdities of my opponents as the sweetest exercise of faith, consoled by the Word of the Gospel "If they kept my word, they will keep yours also" [John 15:20]. If they perverted the Word of Christ, they will also pervert my word. I know that the Word of the Lord does not return empty [Isa. 55:11]. I know that the eyes of the Lord are in every place, keeping watch on the evil and the good [Prov. 15:3]. . . . I beg you not to lend your ears to those who speak against me. Do not believe those who have called me an inconsistent, acrimonious man and who have dishonored me with a thousand other epithets. I don't care a hoot about that; all of this is most pleasing to me, for Christ's sake.[7]

Müntzer added that he anticipated more conflicts but was confident that God would end all of it well. He claimed that the city council and citizens supported him, that he would appeal to a general council of the church to deal with "these birds of prey who tear everything to pieces,"[8] just as Luther had done. He also told Luther that he was quite willing to give an account of his faith to the bishop of Naumburg, and offered to present all his sermons for inspection: "If they were to find anything in them contrary to Christian modesty, I would correct matters."[9]

> If you so suggest, I shall respond to all my superiors. If there is to be an appeal, just write. Whatever you advise, I shall do in the Lord.[10]

Müntzer summarized for Luther what he had heard his opponents say about the Zwickau conflict. The principal issue, he wrote, was that he was preaching "nothing but the Gospel." His chief opponent was the Franciscan Tiburtius, who accused Müntzer of heresy because he used the gospel to oppose human

6. MSB 357:15—358:13.
7. MSB 358:13–17,19–22.
8. MSB 358:22–27.
9. MSB 359:1–2.
10. MSB 359:5–7.

commandments that, according to Tiburtius, must be added to the gospel.

According to Müntzer, the crux of the issue was the relation of Christ to his followers, who must be transformed by imitating his example of suffering and dying. Here Müntzer probably drew on his study of the German mystics and on his acquaintance with Luther's early writings, since they make frequent reference to internal mortification and to what Luther called "turmoil" *(Anfechtung)* or "temptation" *(tentatio)*.[11] Müntzer contrasted this experience of internal mortification to the monastic ideal of poverty, which he considered as ineffective as the external obeisance of the Mass, but which Tiburtius praised as a means of avoiding suffering in the world. Müntzer insisted that he himself preached about the certainty of a faith, anchored in divine predestination which assured salvation, not obedience to human mandates purported to stem from God. He proclaimed salvation by faith, whereas Tiburtius referred to a supernatural reality when speaking of "eternal blessedness":

> With all my heart I have admonished this father of the Franciscan order, Tiburtius of Weissenfels, not to spread among the people such grave errors concerning the salvation of souls, or else to give me and the city council an account of his faith with reliable scriptural passages and the right understanding of them. But he, more cruel than some wild animal, said that he would do neither the one nor the other. Instead, he confidently asserted that I would be annihilated by the whole order; and the raging warrior [like the ancient charioteers], climbed on his chariot full of slander. I ridiculed his rage, and I fear nothing, even if the whole crowd of mendicants should move against me, tear me apart, and butcher me. I am not doing my own work but that of the Lord.[12]

Müntzer then assured Luther that he would stand fast, no matter what the opposition did, and that he would protect the name of the Lord from being slandered by "those whose feet are swift to shed blood" (Rom. 3:15). He added that he would refute these accusations in writing, if Luther so advised:

11. E, 82–85 suggests that Müntzer had read some of Luther's writings of 1519. There is no hard evidence for such a suggestion, despite the fact that Müntzer sounds like Luther in some of his statements.

12. MSB 360:4–11.

Tell me what appears to be Christian to you in all of this. I am most confident, given my previous dangerous experience [at Jüterbog] that I am being singled out for other battles in the world. He who saved me from the most pernicious swamp will save me from the hand [sic] of the beast, the lion and the dragon, so that I shall have no fear though I wander in the midst of the shadow of death. For the Lord is with me, the ever so strong warrior. He will give me a tongue and a wisdom which none of our adversaries will be able to withstand. What more could I desire?[13]

Müntzer closed with greetings to Luther, "You model and lamp to the friends of God," and signed "Thomas Müntzer whom you have conceived in the gospel."[14]

Müntzer certainly wanted Luther to know that he had acted as a supporter of the reform movement and that he acknowledged Luther as one whose advice is cherished. Yet it is not certain that this letter was sent. If so, Luther's reaction is not recorded.[15]

But Müntzer did have the support of the city council, which sent a letter to John of Saxony (brother of the Elector Frederick) asking him to take measures against the Franciscans so that the "preachers of the gospel" could carry on without impediments.[16] Perhaps as a response to this request, the Saxon court finally called representatives of the quarrelling parties together at a meeting chaired by commissioners of the Saxon court on August 25, 1520. Müntzer was told to tone down his rhetoric, and the city council was advised to do its best to keep the peace.[17] Some of Zwickau's influential citizens, such as the former mayor Erasmus Stuler, had gone to confession in Müntzer's church. They supported him because he supported the Lutheran

13. MSB 361:2–8. The words echo biblical passages such as 2 Tim. 4:17, Ps. 22:4–5, Jer. 20:11, and Acts 6:10.

14. MSB 461:8, 10. The signature has been successfully reconstructed by the editor: *"Tomas Munczer qu[em] g[en]u[isti] p[er] evangelium."*

15. MSB 357:11—361:10. The editor speculates that the letter did arrive in Wittenberg. E, 97 surmises that the Zwickau city council had political difficulties with the proposals advocated in the letter, but E does not speculate about the mailing or receipt of the letter itself.

16. The Weimar archives record the basic intention of the letter, which is no longer extant. See E, 98–99.

17. Evidence of the meeting is contained in the Weimar archives. Details in E, 100–101.

movement, and they wanted to be in Luther's camp.[18] When Egranus returned in the fall, the city council called Müntzer as pastor to St. Catherine's, a position that had become available on October 1. There now seemed to be two solid supporters of the reform movement among the preachers in the "Pearl of Saxony." Luther even dedicated his treatise on Christian liberty to the Zwickau mayor, Hermann Mühlphordt, whom Egranus had referred to as one of Luther's supporters. In the "letter of dedication" Luther referred to Egranus as a "learned and wise sir and gracious friend . . . a praiseworthy preacher," but did not mention Müntzer.[19]

Müntzer used his now solid position as pastor of St. Catherine's to test the waters of the Reformation. He quickly sensed that Egranus was the kind of intellectual who could not make up his mind whether to stay with Rome or join Luther's reform movement. As an Erasmian humanist, Egranus had difficulties with Luther's basic theological assertions, especially with the heavy Augustinian emphasis on sin which seemed to leave little, if any, room for human freedom in the salvation process. Moreover, Egranus felt uncomfortable to be associated with someone who attacked tradition, especially the papacy's exclusive teaching authority. When Egranus learned in December 1520 that Luther's archenemy John Eck had cited him as one of Luther's adherents who should be placed under papal ban, he got cold feet and resigned from his call at St. Mary's. Müntzer proposed his Jüterbog friend, Franz Günther, as Egranus's successor, but Günther could not leave his parish in Lochau.[20]

Müntzer quickly made it clear that Catholics should no longer be tolerated in Zwickau. He urged his congregants to do something about the presence of priests and monks in town, and on December 26, 1520, they did. A priest was stoned and almost

18. On September 3, 1520, Stuler wrote a letter to the court chaplain of Elector Frederick, George Spalatin, requesting protection for the Lutheran preachers against the Catholics, especially the Franciscans. E, 102 contains excerpts from a 1799 Latin text.

19. *The Freedom of a Christian*, 1520. WA 7:20.7–8; LW 31:333.

20. The resignation of Egranus and the negotiations with Günther are recorded in the minutes of the Zwickau city council, December 15. E, 110. For an analysis of the differences between Egranus and Luther, see E, 105–9.

lost his life. It happened on St. Stephen's Day, the commemoration of the first Christian martyr, a victim of stoning. John Agricola, one of Müntzer's Wittenberg friends, had tried as early as November to persuade Müntzer to be less aggressive, especially against Egranus.[21] But Müntzer would not be hindered in his campaign to turn Zwickau away from Catholicism. When an official of the Saxon court asked him to explain the violence against a priest, Müntzer, from the pulpit, threatened not only to ban but to stone those who opposed him and the Word of God he preached.[22]

On January 17, 1521, Müntzer wrote a letter to the mayor and the city council of Neustadt, located just west of Zwickau. He requested them to resolve "according to divine law"[23] a pending case regarding the validity of the engagement between a local man and woman. Müntzer had heard that the woman had become engaged to another man, which would be a violation of the law. He admonished the mayor and the council to investigate the matter and report back to him. It is not known whether he was personally acquainted with the couple; nor is it clear how he became involved in the matter. Yet he claimed to have the authority to interfere:

> According to the word of Christ on which the holy church is built, I have seen to it that sad hearts be consoled, just as, a long time ago, God commanded his only Son to do so through Isaiah, and as he spoke through him in Luke 4:18: "The Spirit of the Lord is upon me, to comfort the poor and lonely, and to heal the sick." That is why I have been sent, just as Christ was sent by the Father. We are priests sent from God, according to John 20 [:21] to console poor consciences, unless we are shepherds who only feed themselves (Ezra 34[:2]).[24]

Müntzer claimed that the case had been made more difficult by an ecclesiastical bureaucracy. He believed that the mayor and the council should simply ask the couple for their account of the matter and should not be too hard on the couple.

What is significant in this letter is Müntzer's view of authority,

21. Letter dated November 2, 1520. MSB 362.
22. Recorded in Peter Stulmann's annals. Quoted in E, 113.
23. MSB 366:25, no. 19.
24. MSB 366:3–12.

namely, that the Holy Spirit authorized him to give instructions regarding juridical justice. Standing in the place of Christ, he assumed the same authority granted to bishops in medieval Canon Law. He regarded that law as oppressive, and demanded the use of the higher "spiritual" authority that is given to all those who have the spirit of Christ—presumably also lay people, an interesting interpretation of Luther's concept of the priesthood of all believers. Whereas Luther grounded his views on baptism, and continued to adhere to a distinction between ordination and baptism, Müntzer adopted a spiritualism that no longer distinguished between external orders. Moreover, Müntzer viewed the existing ecclesiastical hierarchy as an impediment to divine justice, and he called on the authorities of Neustadt to ignore the institutional church.

Müntzer's preaching in Zwickau also revived Hussite ideas which had been nurtured for more than a century in Bohemia. Following the execution of the Czech nationalist priest John Hus, who was burned at the stake in Constance in 1415, small groups of sympathizers met in Saxony in so-called conventicles. Some Zwickauers had been Hussites since 1462; they had occasionally been involved in minor acts of violence against Catholic priests. Nicholas Storch, a descendant of a once-prominent family of weavers, had become a leading Hussite sympathizer in Zwickau by 1520. Storch, labeled a "Zwickau prophet" by opponents, apparently taught ideas reflecting millennialist-apocalyptic notions such as the imminent end of the world and denied all external means of salvation, including Scripture, sacraments, and even the institutional church. Müntzer may have been attracted to Storch and his adherents, but he kept a critical distance between himself and the Storchian conventicles and later denied having been influenced by these "Zwickau prophets."[25]

25. In a letter dated July 9, 1523, Müntzer wrote Luther that he himself feared the divine judgment that Nicholas Storch and his companion Marcus Stübner would have to face. MSB 391:21–23. Nevertheless, one can assume a mutual influence. See Siegfried Hoyer, "Die Zwickauer Storchianer—Vorläufer der Täufer?" *Jahrbuch für Regionalgeschichte* 13 (1986): 78. There are only polemical accounts of the Zwickau prophets, and they focus on Storch and Müntzer. It is possible that Storch knew and was perhaps influenced by the Taborites—the radical wing of Hussites which leaned toward apocalyptic views. However, one should not rely too much on the existing polemical accounts.

The lines between a Müntzer faction and the adherents to the old religion and friends of Egranus were clearly drawn during the 1522 pre-Lenten season, the German carnival season, which is traditionally devoted to fun at the expense of others. Almost everyone in town except Egranus himself, who regarded the struggle to be beneath his dignity, participated in various exchanges ranging from slogans to satirical doggerel. One example of the kind of poetry disseminated during that time is:

> O Thomas, you very paragon,
> When evil spirits egg you on
> You preach the cross with much ado.
> Take care the devil not get you![26]

Müntzer's own wit is displayed in twenty-four theses he composed in the spring of 1521 and later published under the title *Propositions of an Excellent Man Named Egranus*.[27] He obviously intended to demonstrate that Egranus was too much of a coward to debate the issues in Zwickau and that, as a theologian, he was not on the side of the angels. "I shall maintain these propositions against the entire world," Müntzer had Egranus say at the end, "particularly against that ass Thomas Müntzer."[28]

The first seven propositions deal with the experiencing of faith. Müntzer had Egranus state that:

1. Christ is not the savior of all those who lived before Him, especially Jews and Gentiles.
2. Christ's earthly suffering does not have to be shared by his followers after his death.
3. Those who lived before Christ contribute to their salvation through excellent moral power.

In these three propositions Egranus appears as a defender of the liberal, scholastic-humanistic tradition that assumes salvific human power without Christ and views grace as timeless, effective in the Old Testament as well as in the New Testament. Müntzer, of course, held the opposite view: Salvation comes

---

26. Document No. 5 in Johann K. Seidemann, *Thomas Müntzer* (Leipzig and Dresden: Arnoldische Buchhandlung, 1842).

27. Text in MSB 513—15. E, 132—66 contains an excellent analysis of the theses, the best feature of the work. Much of my summary is based on this analysis.

28. MSB 515:15–16.

through Christ alone, beginning with his existence in time, and faith in him means participation in his suffering and death.

In propositions (4) through (7) Müntzer had Egranus argue that:

4. The Eucharist, like circumcision, is only "a mere sign," a memorial of Christ's death with no power to forgive sin or to grant the gift of the Holy Spirit.
5. Christ's passion strengthens the human salvific disposition and points to a sweet death that separates the immortal soul from the body.
6. "Contrition of the heart" is sufficient for the forgiveness of sin.
7. The experience of faith is based on an acknowledgment of what Scripture and other books have to say, and unlearned lay persons need not worry about the deeper meaning of faith.

In these four propositions, Egranus is depicted as a rationalist, who relates faith to doctrines rather than seeing it as total commitment to Christ. According to Müntzer, to experience total commitment to Christ means participating in his suffering until one is released from earthly life by way of a bitter death.

The next nine propositions, (8) through (16), deal with questions of the interpretation of Holy Scripture.

8. The Old Testament is valid only for Jews and need not be accepted by Christians.
9. The New Testament must be understood literally.
10. When the Lord's Supper is spoken of as "daily bread" it does not mean that Christ is the "living bread."
11. One part of Scripture cannot be interpreted through another part, but each part must be seen in its independent, historical particularity.

Müntzer had Egranus go on to say that:

12. St. Paul deals mostly with Jews and Gentiles, which is no longer pertinent.
13. Contrary to what Lutherans claim, the Book of Romans is irrelevant because it deals with Jews.
14. Although Romans 8 states that people are totally free of the law, including the Decalogue and its requirements

regarding the Sabbath, it is the gospel, not the law, that reveals sin.

15. One should not fill hearts with the fear of God because the New Testament, through perfect love, drives out all fear.

16. The Gospel of Mark has an apocryphal final chapter, which means that Mark was not a witness to Christ's resurrection.

Thus Müntzer has Egranus exegete Scripture according to its "historical" or "literal" sense and omit the "spiritual sense" completely. That is, Egranus omits the view held by Müntzer that the Holy Spirit cooperates in the interpretation of Scripture.

The final set of propositions, (17) through (24), deals with Egranus's theological method, especially concerning the work of the Holy Spirit. Müntzer insisted that as a rationalist Egranus contended:

17. One is obliged to believe only what one is able to understand, for human reason is all that is necessary to make decisions on matters of faith rather than to be enslaved by irrational faith.

Müntzer added a satirical note: "There has not been anyone more learned in four hundred years than Egranus."[29] In Egranus's view, claimed Müntzer,

18. Human beings have free will, and salvation is effected by human and divine cooperation.

19. An example of such cooperation is Abraham, who was called "father of all nations" because of his superior morality.

20. Only the uneducated call Pelagians heretics, who are better Christians than crude Augustine and all the "Martinians" who follow him, because Pelagians preach that one is saved or damned on the basis of freely made decisions.

21. Only the apostles had the Holy Spirit and their work so stabilized the church that other people do not need the Holy Spirit.

22. No one has had the Holy Spirit in a thousand years, and the church is not governed by it.

29. MSB 514:36–37.

23. There are "four spirits" (a reference to the fourfold sense of Scripture in medieval exegesis)[30] which are revealed in collections of sermons.

Finally, Müntzer had Egranus say:

24. "When I was in Chemnitz, I was driven by a compelling force to give one spirit my whole consideration; [I had] a passionate drive for flexibility and ultimately for money."[31]

An inverted reading of these twenty-four propositions discloses more of Müntzer's own theological ideas than those of Egranus.[32] Caricature and satire were Müntzer's means of making Egranus look like a theological fool, and of presenting himself as the defender of early Lutheran ideas, though it is difficult to know precisely what Luther taught at this time.[33] Müntzer's assertions do contain a "theology of the cross," but with a significant emphasis on mystical participation in Christ's suffering and on the work of the Holy Spirit within the believer. In addition, Müntzer clings to the traditional ways of interpreting the Bible, again with an emphasis on the intimate relationship between external word and internal experiencing of the Holy Spirit.

One can easily surmise that Müntzer's Zwickau period may have brought him closer to an understanding of the origins and nature of the Christian faith, which had been his principal quest from the beginning of his career as a priest and theologian. His study of the German mystics, particularly Tauler, and the digestion of much of Luther's thought certainly helped him to formulate his own ideas. But he did not confine himself just to preaching his ideas from the pulpit of St. Catherine's. He also organized resistance to those who, like Egranus, defended a

30. Nicholas of Lyra (ca. 1270–1349) popularized the fourfold sense of Scripture: literal, tropological or moral, anagogical or edifying, and allegorical.

31. MSB 515:13–14. Chemnitz is located northeast of Zwickau. It is now called Karl-Marx-Stadt.

32. A detailed comparison of what Müntzer presented as Egranian with what Egranus actually taught reveals a significant divergence. See E, 132–66.

33. Rupp, *Patterns of Reformation*, 164, sees many of the propositions as "Martinian doctrines reversed," and observes that Müntzer also shared with Luther and his disciples "a bitter anticlericalism" in his sermons. But definite conclusions cannot be drawn from the evidence of 1520–21.

status quo against the notion that Christians must relate their faith to the affairs of society. There is insufficient evidence to reveal how well Müntzer succeeded in organizing the common people in their conflict against the middle class and nobility of Zwickau, but there was certainly much agitation in the city.[34] The city council minutes record that followers of Müntzer distributed a number of leaflets, among them an "Epistle of the Twelve Apostles and Seventy-two Disciples," which accused Egranus of being a lackey to the rich "big shots" *(grosse Hansen)* who bribe him with gifts and money to preach what they want to hear.[35] Under the leadership of Nicholas Storch, weavers and miners from the silver mines seem to have met quite often to plot various attacks on Catholics and Egranians. Müntzer was not immune: on Shrove Tuesday (February 12) 1521, someone threw rocks through his windows; and someone set a fire in his parsonage on April 10.[36] But he did not stop agitating, in his sermons, against those he considered enemies of the truth, and he seems to have been involved in some demonstrations that resulted in the arrest of some weavers and miners.

Egranus's response to all this was a letter mockingly advising Müntzer to continue his attacks; he himself would keep out of the fray and hope that God would end it well.[37] But on April 16, 1521, after Müntzer and fifty-six weavers created a "tumult," according to some sources, the city council asked him to leave the city. Müntzer denied having had anything to do with the disturbance; he later claimed that he had been taking a bath when the "tumult" occurred. He also claimed he had calmed down the weavers: "If I had not interfered, the whole city council might have been killed the following night [April 17] after the tumult."[38]

On the day Luther triumphantly entered the city of Worms to

34. This is the conclusion of a scholar who knows the existing sources well. See Siegfried Bräuer, "Thomas Müntzers Weg in den Bauernkrieg" in *Thomas Müntzer. Anfragen an die Theologie und Kirche*, ed. Christoph Demke, on behalf of the Secretariat of the Federation of Evangelical Churches in the German Democratic Republic (Berlin: Evangelische Verlagsanstalt, 1977), 87.

35. "Brief der 12 Aposteln und 72 Jünger." Text in Seidemann, op. cit., 110–12.

36. Recorded in the city council minutes. See E, 120.

37. Letter perhaps written in February 1521. MSB 367—68.

38. Letter to Luther dated July 9, 1523. MSB 390:2–5.

face emperor and papal powers, Müntzer left Zwickau. He may have decided to leave in order to defuse a dangerous situation; a pamphlet disseminated by his enemies averred he had fled "under cover of darkness" *(bei Nacht und Nebel).*[39]

39. Quoted in E, 176.

3

A THEOCRATIC MANIFESTO

Shortly after his departure from Zwickau, Müntzer was seen in Saaz (Zatec), across the Saxon border in the kingdom of Bohemia. If there was any region within the Holy Roman Empire where Müntzer could hope to gain strong support for a reform program more radical than Luther's, it was in this Hussite country. For seventeen years (1419–36) after John Hus had been martyred by the Council of Constance in 1415, the radical Hussite faction—the Taborites, named after their stronghold Tabor in southeastern Bohemia—had fought the imperial forces. They had remained undefeated and had rejected a compromise Emperor Sigismund offered to the Utraquist faction of the Hussites (also known as Calixtinians, from *utra*, "both," and *calix*, "chalice") which granted them communion of both kinds, bread and cup, and the right to elect their own archbishop. But in 1453 George of Podebrady, a skilled Utraquist diplomat and military strategist, forced the Taborites to surrender.

When he became king of Bohemia in 1458, George recognized the remaining Hussites, mainly Utraquists, as a church. Most members of this church had become pacifists under the leadership of Peter Chelcicky, and were now known as the Unity of the Czech Brethren (*Unitas Fratrorum Bohemorum* or *Jednota*, also "Bohemian" or "Moravian" Brethren).

But by the end of the fifteenth century, quarrels over doctrine and church discipline plagued the Brethren church. A "minor party" taught abstention from world affairs, based itself on a literal interpretation of the Sermon of the Mount, and rebaptized new members. Under the leadership of Luke of Prague (1460–1528) the "major party," in the majority, managed to prevent a complete schism.[1] Luke of Prague sympathized with Luther's cause. Luther had been called a Hussite at the Leipzig debate in 1519, and many Hussites called Luther the John Hus of Saxony.[2]

Since the Emperor Charles V had had Luther condemned through the Edict of Worms in May 1521, Müntzer undoubtedly felt that Bohemia might become the new center of the Reformation. There were rumors that Luther had been killed, so Müntzer felt that if Luther was known as the John Hus of Saxony, he himself might come to be considered the Martin Luther of Bohemia. He was quite familiar with the Hussite tradition, having studied the records of the Council of Constance, which included details of John Hus's trial and martyrdom. He had also learned more about Hussites from the Zwickauer lay leader Nicholas Storch and other Zwickauers who had been influenced by the Bohemian Hussites.

There were two good reasons for Müntzer to go to Saaz: he was acquainted with the young teacher Mikulas Cernobyl (known as Artemisius), having met him in Wittenberg;[3] and Zwickau businessmen had good connections with Saaz, which was a Bohemian trading center. He could count on finding a strong group of Hussites there. Müntzer stayed in Saaz and its vicinity from the end of April to the beginning of June 1521.[4] He

1. The Podebradian age is well portrayed in Frederick G. Heymann, *George of Bohemia: King of Heretics* (Princeton: Princeton University Press, 1965), esp. chap. 3. See also Harrison S. Thompson, *Czechoslovakia in European History* (Princeton: Princeton University Press, 1953). For an account of Taborite doctrine, see Karl A. Konstantin von Höfer, ed., *Geschichte der hussitischen Bewegung in Böhmen*, 3 vols. (Vienna: Hof und Staatsdruckerei, 1856–1866), 2:434–41. Seventeen theses of Taborite doctrine are quoted from a Catholic source. The struggle over doctrine and discipline among Hussites is analyzed in Peter Brock, *The Political and Social Doctrines of the Unity of the Czech Brethren in the Fifteenth and Early Sixteenth Centuries*, Slavic Printings and Reprintings 11, ed. Cornelius H. van Schooneveld, (The Hague: Mouton Press, 1971), esp. chaps. 3—4.

2. In a letter dated July 17, 1519, Ladislas Rozdalowsky, provost of Prague University, told Luther "what John Hus was formerly in Bohemia, that you are, Martin Luther, in Saxony." WA.BR 1:420.38–39. LC 1:199.

3. See Václav Husa, *Thomáš Müntzer a Čechy*, Rozpravy Československe Akademie Věd 67, no. 11 (Prague, 1957), 51–52.

4. Müntzer may have made more than one trip to Bohemia, but it is difficult to determine. I am following the reasonable analysis of the sources in E, 183–84.

was contemplating a journey to Prague, since Saaz Hussites had contacts with the leaders of the Czech Brethren there.

But first Müntzer returned to Saxony to visit Marcus Thomae. Called Stübner because his father owned a bath house *(Badestube)*, Thomae was a former Wittenberg student living in Elsterberg, just southwest of Zwickau. Müntzer had probably become acquainted with Thomae during his stay in Wittenberg in 1518. At any rate, Müntzer planned to take Marcus Thomae with him to Prague, along with one of his fervent disciples, Hans Löbe "the Bohemian"; Löbe, however, felt called to stay in Zwickau and refused to go along as Müntzer's interpreter.[5]

Müntzer was convinced that he had a divine call to Prague. "We can no longer hesitate in our cause," he wrote to Marcus Thomae from Elsterberg. "I have to tell you this again and again, so that Satan does not block our path."[6] On the same day, he sent some personal papers to a friend in Jena, with an accompanying letter saying that he would return from Bohemia the next spring. He added that a last will and testament would follow later, in case something should happen to him during the journey. He quoted St. Paul (1 Cor. 9:22): "To the weak I have become weak so that I might win the weak. I have become all things to all people, so that I might by all means save some of them."[7]

Müntzer also wrote to Nicholas Hausmann, his successor in Zwickau. Hausmann had his hands full coping with the rivaling factions of Müntzerites, Storchites, Catholics, and Egranians. In his letter, Müntzer chided Hausmann for looking down on the common people and instead wooing the upper classes, admonished him to speak out against Egranus, "this evil man," and urged him to bring about a victory for the truly faithful just as the prophet Elijah had done when he fought the priests of Baal (1 Kings 18). He closed by informing Hausmann that he was going to Bohemia not for personal gain or glory but to proclaim "the mystery of the cross" there.[8]

5. Müntzer's letter to Stübner on June 15, 1521, was addressed to Elsterberg, or at least nearby. MSB 369–70. At about the same time, Löbe wrote to Müntzer from Zwickau. MSB 370. See also the reconstruction of the letter in E, 178–79.

6. MSB 370:7, 9–10.

7. Letter to Michael Gans dated June 15, 1521. MSB 371:7–9.

8. MSB 371–73.

When Müntzer and Thomae arrived in Prague on June 21, they were solemnly welcomed as representatives of Luther's reform movement. Prague chroniclers recorded that Müntzer preached at the Bethlehem and Corpus Christi chapels near the university. One of them called him "Magister Thomas Lutheranus," representative of Lutheranism.[9] He also preached in the famous Utraquist Thein Church in the center of the city, and he was a house guest at the well-known Caroline College *(Collegium Carolinum).*

Although there are no detailed accounts of Müntzer's preaching, he probably tried to persuade the Prague intellectuals as well as the common people to accept him as the leader of a reformation intended to complete the work of Hus and Luther. He had brought along a set of Melanchthonian theses expressing Luther's views regarding human righteousness by faith alone, human weakness due to sin, and the authority of Scripture over church and councils. "An emulator of Martin *(emulus Martinia)* before God, 2 half-mile markers before Prague" is a marginal note in Müntzer's handwriting, and indicates that he had brought along the theses for a debate with Prague Hussites and/or Lutherans.[10] There is no evidence that any such debate took place, but chroniclers report that on July 7, the anniversary of John Huss's death, there was a demonstration in memory of John Hus which resulted in the destruction of statues and relics in the Catholic monasteries of St. James and St. Clement.[11] It is not known whether Müntzer and Stübner took an active part in this demonstration.

Müntzer, meanwhile, was receiving reports from Germany informing him that Luther's Reformation had reached a critical

9. Husa, op.cit., 63.

10. The theses are not in MSB, but are included in Heinrich Boehmer and Paul Kirn, eds., *Thomas Müntzers Briefwechsel,* Schriften der sächsischen Kommission für Geschichte 34 (Leipzig, E. Ger.: Teubner, 1931), appendix no. 5. Melanchthon composed them on September 9, 1519, for a disputation fulfilling a requirement for the degree of Baccalaureate of Holy Scripture. Lydia Müller *(Der Kommunismus der mährischen Wiedertäufer,* Schriften des Vereins für Reformationsgeschichte 45, no. 142 [Leipzig, E. Ger.: Heinsius, 1927]) discovered that they had been copied by Müntzer. English summary in Clyde L. Manschreck, *Melanchthon: The Quiet Reformer* (New York and Nashville: Abingdon, 1958), 50–51.

11. Ibid., 63.

stage. One of his friends in Halberstadt wrote him on June 25, 1521, that Luther had been condemned at Worms and that all of his disciples might have to share the same fate.[12] A Zwickau friend reported on rumors of Müntzer's death, and asked for more information regarding his actual situation in Prague.[13] A little later, his Halberstadt friend asked him why Christ could accomplish more in Bohemia than in Germany.[14]

On All Saints Day, November 1, 1521, Müntzer emulated Luther's action of 1517 by posting a manifesto handwritten in German on (perhaps) a door of a centrally located church in Prague. The manifesto presented his views on the religious situation in Bohemia. He followed up this "Prague Manifesto" (he gave it no title) with three revised versions in German, Latin, and Czech.[15] He was obviously attempting to address all strata of Czech society to win their support for what he considered to be the true Reformation. The original German text begins with a personal confession:

> I, Thomas Müntzer of Stolberg, confess before the entire church and world, wherever this letter may be shown, with Christ as my witness, and all the elect who have known me since childhood, that I have used the greatest diligence, more than anyone I have known, to receive a higher instruction about the holy, invincible Christian faith. Throughout my whole life, there has been no monk or priest able to teach me to comprehend (God knows I am not lying) the true exercise of faith, which includes the valuable inner turmoil *(Anfechtung)* which transfigures faith in the spirit of the fear of God—this means that an elect must have the Holy Spirit seven times.[16]

Using the terminology of late medieval German mysticism, Müntzer elaborated upon his experiences with the church of his youth:

12. Letter by Hans Pelt. MSB 374:8–12.
13. Letter dated July 31, 1521, by Hans Sommerschuh. MSB 376:29–31.
14. Letter dated September 6, 1521, from Hans Pelt. MSB 377:11–13.
15. The texts of all four versions are found in MSB 491—511, and were dubbed the Prague Manifesto by the editor. The conjecture that Müntzer may have posted the first German version is based on the size of the sheets of paper he used, 42.5 cm. x 33 cm.—about 2 ft. x 1 ft., which is why some scholars call the document "Prague Poster" *(Prager Anschlag)*. See Bensing, *Thomas Müntzer,* 42. E, 188–213 contains a detailed analysis of all versions.
16. MSB 491:1–11.

Not a single scholar mentioned to me anything at all about the order of God as it is placed into all creatures and about how the whole can be known through all of its parts. All those who claimed to be Christians, especially the accursed priests, were never aware of this. I did, of course, hear about the mere words that they, like murderers and thieves, stole from the Bible. Jeremiah 23[:30] calls such stealing "stealing my words from one another," words they themselves never heard from the mouth of God Himself. I think the devil ordained these fine preachers to do just that! But St. Paul, in 2 Cor. 3[:3] writes that human hearts are the paper or parchment upon which God inscribes with His finger, not with ink, His immovable will and eternal wisdom. This script can be read by anyone whose mind He has opened, just as Jeremiah [31:33] and Ezekiel say [Hos. 6:2–3?]: God writes His law on the third day of His sprinkling. Then human minds will be opened. God does this in His elect from the very beginning, so that they may have not an uncertain but an invincible attestation of the Holy Spirit, who gives our spirit sufficient affirmation that we are children of God. Whoever does not feel the Spirit of Christ inwardly, or indeed does not possess it with certainty, is a member of the devil and not of Christ, in accordance with Rom. 8[:9]. Now the world, confused by many sects, has for a long time longed for the truth, and the saying of Jeremiah has become true: "The children beg for food, but no one gives it to them" [Lam. 4:4]. There have been many, and there are still many today, who throw the bread to them as if to dogs— that is, the word of God in the letter. But they do not break it for them. Oh, mark it well! They do not break it for the children. They do not explain the true spirit of the fear of God, which would have truly taught them that they are irremovable children of God. That is why Christians have become poltroons when sent to defend the truth, prattling splendidly that God no longer speaks with people, just as though He had become dumb. They think it sufficient to read it [the Word of God] in books and spit it out raw, like a stork spits out frogs for its young in the nest. They are not like the hen who gathers her young to keep them warm; they do not put God's good, natural Word into [children's] hearts, like a mother giving milk to a child. Instead, like Balaam [Num. 22—23] they carry the letter in their mouths while their hearts are more than a hundred thousand miles away from it. Because of such foolishness it would not be surprising if God were to shatter us with such a foolish faith. Nor am I surprised that all the generations of people slander and reject us Christians; no one could do otherwise. This is what has been written here and there. Yes, dear lords, there is beautiful proof of it in the chicken coop [sic]. Simple or unbelieving people coming into our assembly would say, "Are you mad? What do we care about your Scripture?"[17]

17. MSB 491:11—493:11.

Müntzer then depicted the stark contrast in God's Word between the dead letter promulgated by ecclesiastical scribes and the living word that transforms people from within:

> But when we are taught the true living word of God, we are able to win over the unbelievers and to know clearly when the secrets of their hearts are revealed, so that they must humbly confess that God is in us. You see, this is what Paul also attests in 1 Corinthians 14, when he says that a preacher must have revelation, for otherwise he cannot preach the word of God. [Even] the devils believe that the Christian faith is correct. If the servants of the Antichrist reject this, then God must indeed be mad and foolish, since He has said that His word shall never perish. Would it not have perished if God had stopped speaking it?
>
> Pay attention to the text if you have a brain in your head: "Heaven and earth will pass away, but my words will not pass away" [Matt. 24:35]. If it is only written in books and God did once say it, and it has disappeared into thin air, then it cannot be the word of the eternal God. It is only a creature, entering memory from the outside. But that is against the true order and against the rule of the holy faith Jeremiah writes about. That is why all prophets must say, "Thus says the Lord," not "Thus has the Lord said" as though it were past; they use the present tense.[18]

According to Müntzer, faith is the result of the direct transmission of divine truth by the Holy Spirit into the human heart and soul. That is why he accused Roman Catholic and Lutheran leaders of propagating a dead faith based on the dead letter of Holy Scripture. He was convinced, mainly by his research in early Christian records, that his "spiritualism" was in agreement with early Christianity.

> I have become thoroughly aware of this unbearable and malicious fault of Christianity by reading through the history of the ancient fathers. I discovered that the immaculate virginal church became a prostitute shortly after the time of the disciples and the apostles through a spiritual adultery brought about by the scholars who always want to sit at the top—as Hegesippus and, after him, Eusebius have written in Book 4, chapter 22 [Ecclesiastical History]. Moreover, I discovered that no ecclesiastical council has given an account of the inviolable Word of God in accordance with the straight, living order. It was all a childish prank. God, in his lenient will, permitted all of this so that all human work might be re-

18. MSB 493:11–30.

vealed. But, God be blessed, it will never happen that the monkish priests will be the Christian church. Instead, as Paul teaches, the elect friends shall also learn to prophesy the Word of God so that they may really experience how amiably—indeed how wholeheartedly—God speaks with all His elect. For God's sake, I am willing to sacrifice my whole life to bring to light such teaching.[19]

Müntzer closed by exhorting the Bohemians not to reject him but to regard him as the prophet who, like Jeremiah, announces the will of God:

God will do marvelous things with his elect, especially in this land. For here shall begin a new church, and this nation will be a mirror for the entire world. That is why I call on everyone to assist me in defending the Word of God. Moreover, through the Holy Spirit I shall demonstrate to you that you have been taught to offer sacrifices to the idol Baal. If you refuse, God will have you slain by the Turks next year. I know that in saying this I speak the truth. I shall suffer for it as Jeremiah suffered. Take it to heart, dear Bohemians. I call not only you but also God Himself to account, as Peter says [Acts 5:29 (?)]. I shall also be accountable to you. If I should fail in this endeavor of which I boast, I shall become a child of temporal and eternal death. I can give you no higher pledge. Christ be with you.[20]

The expanded German and the Latin versions of the manifesto disclose an even more aggressive Müntzer. He accuses the existing church of being run by representatives of Satan who are as hard as stone in their perversion:

Their hearts are harder than flint, which rejects the master's chisel in all eternity. That is why they are called "stone" by our dear Lord. They produce no fruit, even though they receive the dead word with great joy and glory. As Ezekiel indicates [11:19], these stony hearts are those of the priests and the people like them, who delight in their books and say "We are wise and the law of the Lord is with us." . . . That is why the people are forced to live without true shepherds; the experience of faith is never preached to them. They are told that one can escape the wrath of God by doing good works and by acquiring precious virtues, but all of this does not teach them who God is, what true faith is, and what strong virtue

19. MSB 493:31—394:16.
20. MSB 494:17–29.

and good works are. In their spirit of confusion they are unmoved and have become unshaken [Isa. 19:14].[21]

Again and again Müntzer refers to inward suffering *(Anfechtung)* as the prerequisite for true experiencing of faith with the advent of the Holy Spirit in the innermost depth, "in the pit of the soul" *(Seelenabgrund)*. This, according to Müntzer, is the way in which God restores the original order of creation between Creator and creatures, who had enjoyed a most intimate relationship with God before the fall of Adam and Eve. Thus God is ready to make a final move and pour out his Spirit on those who experience the trials and tribulations of the final age.

> O how ripe the rotten apples are! O how tender the elect have become! The time of harvest is at hand! That is why God Himself has hired me for His harvest. I have sharpened my sickle, for my thoughts are focused only on the truth, and my lips, my skin, my hands, my hair, my soul, my body, and my life curse the un-believers.
>
> In order to do my work properly, I have come to your land, my dearest Bohemians. I desire nothing more than that you diligently study the Word of God from His own mouth. Then you will see for yourselves, and hear and grasp how the whole world has been seduced by the dumb priests. For the sake of Christ's blood, help me to fight these enemies of the faith! In the spirit of Ezekiel, I shall disgrace them before your eyes. First in your land, and then every-where else, a new apostolic church will rise.[22]

The grand vision that Müntzer proposed in this Prague man-ifesto was of him, as the last of God's prophets, succeeding "the dear and holy crusader John Hus"[23] and initiating the final age of the world, at which time God would restore the original, sinless order of creation. According to Müntzer, this restoration had already begun when God's Spirit entered the hearts and souls of those chosen to spearhead what was to expand from a holy remnant into a new Apostolic church spreading from Bohemia to the ends of the earth. As promised through the

21. MSB 507:10–15; 508:30—509:5. Latin version.

22. MSB 504:17–31. Expanded German version.

23. So designated in the expanded German version of the manifesto. MSB 495:3.

prophets of the Old Testament and the apostles of the new covenant, God would thus establish eternal rule. God would punish those who rejected Müntzer's final plea through the advancing Turks, the instruments of the antichrist. However, the antichrist, too, would finally have to accede to the eternal lordship of Christ.

This vision is thoroughly theocratic, because it advocates God's rule in place of any other. So it is not surprising that the Prague authorities barred Müntzer from preaching after the publication of his manifesto, placed him under house arrest for a while, and then exiled him from the city.[24] Marcus Stübner later reported that people had tried to stone him, Stübner, after they heard him preach.[25]

Müntzer and Stübner left Prague sometime before Christmas, 1521. Somewhere along the road they parted, and Stübner went alone to Wittenberg to join a certain Thomas Drechsel and Nicholas Storch, who had been causing considerable turmoil in Zwickau after Müntzer's departure. These three, dubbed Zwickau prophets, organized riots in the streets, led attacks against priests during church services, and preached the imminence of the end of the world. Many of Luther's disciples, especially Carlstadt, were quite impressed by them. They began implementing the three so-called prophets' recommendations for a radical reformation of public life, which added to the disturbances in the city. All this finally forced Luther to return from the Wartburg castle. Supported by the city government and Elector Frederick, he succeeded in restoring order with a series of sermons preached during Lent of 1522, every day from March 9 to 16. Luther completely rejected the views of the "Zwickau prophets," whom he regarded as messengers of Satan. The "Zwickau prophets" left Wittenberg shortly after Luther returned there, and were not heard from again.[26]

24. The archives contain few details. Müntzer and Stübner may also have fled to avoid possible persecution. See Husa, *Thomas Müntzer*, 87; E, 213; and Bensing, *Thomas Müntzer*, 43–44, 49, who think it probable that Müntzer fled. Otherwise the four versions of the manifesto would not have been preserved.

25. Stübner's report, according to the Wittenberg archives. See Nikolaus Müller, *Die Wittenberger Bewegung* (Leipzig, E. Ger.: Heinsius, 1911), 160.

26. For a detailed account of the "Wittenberg movement" of 1521–22, and the debate regarding its interpretation, see Rupp, *Patterns of Reformation*, chap. 6.

Müntzer meanwhile was almost constantly on the road, visiting friends, trying to win support for his cause, and seeking employment. He probably stopped in Jena to pick up the private papers he had left with Michael Gans; he wrote some letters from Nordhausen, not too far from Stolberg; and he may have stayed for brief periods in Erfurt, Halle, Weimar, perhaps even Wittenberg.[27]

A letter dated March 27, 1522, addressed to Philip Melanchthon discloses Müntzer's state of mind. Referring to himself as "messenger of Christ" *(nuntius Christi),* he compliments the Wittenbergers: "I wholeheartedly approve of your theology, for it has snatched many souls of the elect from the snares of hunters."[28] However, he then proceeds to criticize Luther and his adherents for neglecting "the living word of God" and its prophetic power. "Believe me, God is more willing to speak than you are prepared to hear."[29] Müntzer uses the examples of clerical marriage and the Mass to illustrate his own views. With regard to clerical marriage, he cites Paul (1 Cor 7:1–7) to argue that such a bond is anchored in the sanctifying work of the Holy Spirit, who endows the children of such a marriage with the power to become the future church. Therefore, he insists, the physical aspects of a clerical marriage must be subordinated to its spiritual sanctification:

> No commandment (if I may say it this way) is more binding on the Christian than sanctification. For it first empties the soul, in accordance to God's will, until the soul can no longer accept the lower pleasures in any way as usurpers; we have wives as though we had none [1 Cor 7:29]. Do not give what you owe like the heathens do.

27. E, chap. 5 offers the best analysis of the evidence. According to E, Müntzer could have travelled from Prague straight northwest to Jena, Erfurt, and Weimar, then on to Nordhausen. Manfred Bensing, "Thomas Müntzer und Nordhausen (Harz) 1522," ZGW 10 (1962): 1095–1123, claims that Müntzer held a pastorate in Nordhausen, but this is unlikely and was refuted by E, 217–18. He may have participated in a disputation in Weimar (E, 237–38), but the date, as well as the link to a fragmentary summary of a Weimar disputation among his writings, make this uncertain (MSB 565; E, 237–39). According to E, 242–43, Müntzer was in the vicinity of Wittenberg in December 1522 and then stayed in Halle until March 1523. In Halle, he served as auxiliary priest *(kaplan)* at St. George Church, with the special responsibility of caring for the spiritual direction of the nuns there (E, 244 and Bensing, *Thomas Müntzer,* 47–48).

28. MSB 380:3–4.

29. MSB 380:18.

> Give like one who knows that God speaks to you, commands you, admonishes you—so that you know with certainty when to give what you owe for the sake of a chosen offspring. That is how the fear of God and the spirit of truth impede your animal lust, so that you are not swallowed up by it.[30]

Müntzer is here responding to one of Luther's 1522 Lenten sermons on the difference between "musts" (such as baptism) and "adiaphora" (things neither commanded nor forbidden in matters of salvation). Clerical marriage is not a "must," Luther had contended, but it is better to rest on a strong and clear text of Scripture than follow the crowd, especially when uncertainty is the diabolic temptation.[31] Such a contention is erroneous, according to Müntzer, because it is based on the "dead letter of Scripture" rather than on the living word of God given through the work of the Holy Spirit in the heart.[32]

Müntzer agrees with the Wittenbergers' call to abolish the papal Mass, but he declares them wrong for doing so on the basis of Scripture and for adopting "the apostolic rite."[33] According to Müntzer, true worship exists and is experienced only by "the elect" who have experienced the Holy Spirit and have thus been separated from those who adhere to the "dead promises" of the dead letter of Scripture.[34] Thus Müntzer argues for an examination of the worshiping community: only those who have experienced the Holy Spirit and can testify to it should be allowed to partake of the Lord's Supper. Luther had simply wanted to avoid offending the weak, but Müntzer maintains, "Our dear Martin acts without knowledge when he wishes not to offend 'children' (parvuli), even though these children have been cursed because they have remained children for a hundred years."[35] The time of waiting for the weak and uninitiated to come around is over:

> Do not hesitate [with the harvest]. The summer is at hand. Do not make friends with those who are reprobates; they are the ones who

30. MSB 380:25—381:4.
31. WA 10/3:22.26—23.25. LW 51:79–80.
32. MSB 380:9.
33. MSB 381:12–13.
34. MSB 381:14–19.
35. MSB 381:20–21.

prevent the word [of God] from working with great power [1 Thess. 2:13]. Do not flatter your princes, or you will experience your own demise, which our blessed God may prevent.[36]

Luther had contended that any changes in public worship should be initiated gradually and only with the support of the government. Müntzer, on the other hand, advocates a worshiping community that is "spiritualized" rather than "politicized," empowered solely by the work of the Holy Spirit. He advances the principle of "by Spirit alone" (without, however, using the slogan *solo spiritu*) against that of "by Scripture alone" *(sola Scriptura)* of the Wittenbergers.

Müntzer briefly refers to the doctrine of purgatory as an undesirable way of speaking of the purification of Christians. While agreeing with the Wittenbergers' rejection of the doctrine, he nevertheless reminds them again that Christians must experience spiritual purification through *Anfechtung* and the Spirit before they can belong to the true church.[37] This theocratic, spiritualistic, and charismatic stance is what separated Müntzer from Luther and his adherents.

Using German rather than Latin, Müntzer ends his letter, "You tender scribes, do not get upset. I cannot do otherwise."[38] It sounds like a farewell from one who owes much to Luther but who feels they have come to a parting of the ways.

Müntzer felt that his cause was opposed, especially by territorial rulers, wherever he went. "These inane lords lie," he wrote from Nordhausen,

> if they babble that I invalidate the doctrine of Christ (as they call it). I place the immutable will of God, to which I have always adhered, against their claims. I am totally committed to exhibiting the church of Jesus Christ in its essence, predetermined by God, to all the godless impostors. What does it matter if they complain that spiritual people have become confused and uncertain? Dangerous times are ahead for all the godless. But, based on their own questionable conclusions, they feel important, as though they had been especially distinguished by divine grace—of which they know as much as a goose knows about the sky's Milky Way.[39]

36. MSB 381:23–26.
37. MSB 381:27—382:2.
38. MSB 382:2–3.
39. Letter dated July 14, 1522, from Nordhausen. MSB 384:28—385.5.

He went on to explain that God allows people some time to experience the Holy Spirit in their souls, and thereby to discern God's will, but that there would be a final reckoning. He signed the letter "Thomas Müntzer, the son who shakes out the wicked" [Job 38:13].[40]

After a miserable winter, which he survived with the help of friends, Müntzer was more eager than ever to find a position as pastor. On March 19, 1523, he mentioned his expulsion from Halle to friends there, without stating any reasons;[41] by Easter of 1523, he was made a probationary pastor at St. John's in Allstedt, a small town on the western border of electoral Saxony, between Leipzig and Halle.

40. MSB 385:21.
41. MSB 388:13.

4

A BASE FOR ACTION

Allstedt was a small and insignificant town, under the jurisdiction of Elector Frederick the Wise. The townspeople, mostly farmers, and miners who worked in the iron mines in nearby Mansfeld, lived withdrawn from the world. They knew little, if anything, about the events that shaped their time, be it the threat of the Turkish invasion or imperial power politics.[1] The town council knew that the elector did not oppose the new reform movement, which favored lay participation in the affairs of the church. The priest of St. Wiprecht's Church, Simon Haferitz, had an interest in Luther's reform movement without, however, creating any excitement about it.

Since the Allstedt leaders leaned toward the new movement, they invited Müntzer to come for a probationary period as pastor to St. John's Church, which lacked a pastor at the time. Müntzer would eventually have to be duly elected and certified by Elector Frederick in accordance with the law of Saxon patronage. There is some evidence that Müntzer may have been recommended for this position by a noblewoman, Felicitas of Selmenitz, who had come to know and to like Müntzer when he

1. Information on Allstedt is not extensive. Archival sources have not yet been fully researched. There is a useful summary of dates as well as of research in Siegfried Bräuer, "Thomas Müntzer und der Allstedter Bund" in Jean-Georges Rott and Simon L. Verheus, eds., *Täufertum und radikale Reformation im 16. Jahrhundert*, Akten des internationalen Kolloquiums für Täufergeschichte des 16. Jahrhundets gehalten in Verbindung mit der 11. Mennonitischen Weltkonferenz in Strassburg, Juli 1984 (Baden-Baden, 1987), 85–87. See also A. Nebe, "Geschichte des Schlosses und der Stadt Allstedt," HZ 20 (1887): 18–95.

served St. George's Church in Halle.[2] In any event, the town council apparently favored him because of his reputation as a well-educated supporter of ecclesiastical reform.

Müntzer seemed eager to settle down and realize some of his own plans for renewing the church. He married Ottilie of Gersen, an apostate nun, possibly just before or just after his arrival in Allstedt, since the records show the birth of a son on March 27, 1524, Easter Sunday, one year after he assumed his duties at St. John's on Easter Sunday, April 5, 1523. Hardly anything is known as to how Müntzer met, or why he married, Ottilie. She became a faithful supporter of his cause, and helped him care for his father, who moved in with them in 1523 and died a year later.[3]

Müntzer began a program of liturgical reform designed to involve the common people in the life of the church. This program focused on the translation of biblical texts and a musicological rearrangement of the orders of worship, which included hymns. It was the first "Protestant" effort and predated Luther's liturgical reforms in Wittenberg.[4] Müntzer first created a *German Church Order (Deutsches Kirchenamt)* with the revealing subtitle "Instituted for the purpose of lifting the perfidious cover that hid from the world the light now shining again in these hymns of praise and divine psalms, for the edification of a growing Christendom, conforming to God's immutable will for the annihilation of the ostentatious deportment of the godless."[5]

The new order was to be used during the five major seasons of the church year: Advent, Christmas, Lent, Easter, and Pentecost. Müntzer did not change the basic structure of the church order;

---

2. The evidence is circumstantial and is overrated by Bensing (*Thomas Müntzer,* 47) who concluded that Felicitas of Selmenitz was responsible for Müntzer's move to Allstedt. E, 242–43, 249, leaves the question open. Bräuer ("Thomas Müntzer und der Allstedter Bund," 87, n. 15) rejects the thesis of Felicitas's influence, which was first advanced by Karl Honemeyer, "Müntzers Berufung nach Allstedt," HZ 16 (1964): 107–8.

3. E, 374–79 analyzed the scanty evidence without coming to any definite conclusions.

4. Luther's revision of public worship began later in 1523. See the introduction to and collection of Luther's liturgical writings in LW 53. Müntzer's work has been carefully analyzed in E, 252–360, and includes a musicological assessment by Henning Frederichs (ibid., 339–60).

5. MSB 25. Entire text, 30–155.

he merely simplified and reduced it, to make sure that the laity appreciated the work of the Holy Spirit through Christ and would not be sidetracked by such practices as the invocation of Mary or the cult of the saints. According to Müntzer, the five major seasons provided an opportunity "to sing the entire Bible," beginning with the birth of Christ and ending with the advent of the Holy Spirit at Pentecost. "Thus Christ is transfigured in us through the Holy Spirit and His testimony of how He was proclaimed by the prophets, was born, died, and was resurrected; He rules with the Father and the same Holy Spirit forever, and makes us His disciples."[6]

Müntzer next transformed the existing order of the Roman Mass into a *German Evangelical Mass (Deutsch-Evangelische Messe)*, using Luther's translation of the Gospels and his own translation of the Psalms, and fitting them into a framework of congregational singing based on the Gregorian chant.[7] In his preface, he again makes clear that people can only worship truly if they are "the chosen friends of God." This mystical description was later to be used for the "League of the Elect."[8] The Psalms were intended to prepare the congregation for true worship and were to be read and sung by the laity.

> In them [the Psalms] is the work of the Holy Spirit clearly recognized, as to what attitude one should have toward God and how to come to the advent of the true Christian faith. All this is clearly said about the Holy Spirit in the Psalms.[9]

Such liturgical practice was designed to separate believers from the hypocrisy of the Roman Church and makes them "Christshaped" *(christförmig)*.[10]

Finally, Müntzer published *The German Church Order of Allstedt (Ordnung und Berechnung des Deutschen Amtes zu Allstedt)*, which consists of instructions for the order of Sunday public worship and for baptism, weddings, communion of the sick, and burial of the dead.[11] Again stressing the edification of the whole

6. MSB 162:32–35.
7. Text in MSB 162—206.
8. MSB 163:2.
9. MSB 164:22–26.
10. MSB 165:7–10.
11. Text in MSB 208—15.

congregation, he linked his proposals for liturgical reform to his mystical and spiritualist theology: He, like the others among God's elect, had the "key to God's knowledge" *(Kunst Gottes)*. God enters the heart of the believer through the living Word; public worship is a way to obtain such a personal experience.[12] Given the variety of historical and cultural contexts, the details of public worship may change, but the movement toward true faith must occur in all worship services—in Allstedt or anywhere else. "Be filled with the Holy Spirit, and address one another in Psalms and hymns and spiritual songs" (Eph. 5:18–19).[13] But Müntzer proposed no radical changes in the order of baptism, even though he later criticized the baptism of infants. His intention was simply to be more "evangelical," that is, to focus on theocentric worship, an act of thanksgiving climaxing in the Eucharist. The task of involving and therefore edifying the entire congregation had to be done in the German language. These liturgical reforms reveal Müntzer's aesthetic sensitivity, musical pathos, and application of specific theological ideas.

Erfurt and some other cities moved to adopt his new liturgies in 1525, but refrained from doing so when they learned of the author's involvement in the peasants' rebellion and his execution in 1525. Yet even the liturgical reform efforts Luther instituted in Wittenberg may have been precipitated because of the new Allstedt liturgies.[14]

Müntzer's preaching soon attracted large crowds. Within a few weeks of his arrival, people were journeying from the surrounding villages and towns to hear the new preacher. At one time he attracted two thousand visitors, some from as far away as Halle.[15] Simon Haferitz, the other pastor in town, made common cause with him, and between the liturgical reforms and Müntzer's preaching, Allstedt was becoming the center of a

12. MSB 208:6–16.

13. MSB 214:3–6.

14. The positive and negative aspects of Müntzer's liturgical reform have been summarized by Siegfried Bräuer, "Thomas Müntzers Liedschaffen," LJ 41 (1974): 45–102. On Müntzer's influence on Luther, 101–102.

15. Reported by the electoral official in Allstedt to Frederick the Wise on April 11, 1524. Quoted in Bräuer, "Müntzers Liedschaffen," 47.

popular movement. The Catholic monasteries in the country-side, however, criticized him heavily.

Müntzer tried to maintain contact with Luther. Addressing Luther as "Most honorable father" *(sincerissimus pater)*, he pleaded a common cause with him in a letter dated July 9, 1523. He did, however, complain about the treatment he had been given in Zwickau:

> Never has my feeling for your love been so cheap that I would have lent an ear to cheap insinuations [about you]. I have known from the very beginning that you did not plead your own cause but rather that of all people. But I was terribly upset when in your letter you recommended to me this most pestilential Egranus.[16]

This was a reminder that he had seen, much earlier than Luther, the kind of person Egranus was. He then went on to explain his position on revelation, particularly his views on the work of the Holy Spirit, on visions, and on dreams and their relation to Scripture. He told Luther that the centerpiece of the doctrine on revelation is the notion that true Christianity is grounded in the Holy Spirit's testimony in the believer. Only those who "have been taught from the mouth of the living God" know that Christ's teaching is not a human invention but the loving God's gift.[17]

Müntzer cited Scriptural passages such as Isa. 8:19–20 and John 7:17, which refer to visions and to recognition of God's Word, to support his claim that dreams and visions are appropriate means of revelation. He was aware of Luther's antagonism to such a view, so he assured him that he only relied on visions and dreams whenever they did not contradict God's word in the testimony of Scripture, adding "Dearest patron, you have come to know Thomas."[18] In other words, he hoped that Luther knew him well enough not to charge him with teaching strange doctrines, since Scripture itself grants validity to prophetic visions and raptures. "I am not so arrogant that I would refuse to be corrected and taught better by your superior testimony so that we could follow the path of love together."[19]

16. MSB 389:16–20.
17. MSB 390:8–12.
18. MSB 391:7–8.
19. MSB 391:19–21.

In this letter, Müntzer insisted that he had nothing in common with the "Zwickau prophets," referring to Storch and Stübner by name.[20] But he did defend his use of mystical terminology, despite the fact that Luther might find it "nauseating": "Best father, I do know the rule the apostle [Paul] has given to avoid profane and unusual phrases as well as boasting with false knowledge. Believe me, I have no intention of saying anything I cannot verify with a clear text of Scripture."[21] He declared himself eager to restore their friendship and to remain in the fellowship of those who led the movement. "May the Lord protect you and restore the old love," he concluded, adding greetings to Melanchthon and other friends.[22]

Luther's response to the letter was negative and indirect. He wrote to the Allstedt leaders advising them to withdraw their support of Müntzer and accusing him of shunning debate and of abusing Scripture.[23] The political unrest caused by the Zwickau prophets in Wittenberg while he was at the Wartburg and Müntzer's activities in Zwickau had made Luther nervous; he hated chaos and had already warned against engaging in rebellious activities.[24]

The fact that Luther and the Wittenbergers linked his name to violence and rebellion was of great concern to Müntzer. He had left both Zwickau and Prague at the onset of unrest, even though his inflammatory preaching style had been partly to blame. His listeners seemed confused as to the difference between internal turmoil caused by the Holy Spirit and external rebellion against ecclesiastical hypocrisy and political injustice. Müntzer therefore wrote *An Honest Open Letter to His Dear Brethren in Stolberg to Avoid Illegitimate Rebellion* on July 18, 1523, in order to explain his position more clearly.[25]

20. MSB 391:21–23.

21. MSB 391:25–27.

22. MSB 391:28—392:1.

23. Letter to George Spalatin, dated August 3, 1523. WA. BR 3:120.

24. See *A Sincere Admonition to All Christians to Guard against Insurrection and Rebellion* 1522. WA 8:676–87. LW 45:57–74.

25. MSB 21–22. This is a difficult text. One of the better editions is in Siegfried Bräuer and Wolfgang Ullmann, eds., *Thomas Müntzer, Theologische Schriften aus dem Jahr 1523*, 2d ed. (Berlin: Evangelische Verlagsanstalt, 1982), 67–70. English translation by Michael G. Baylor, "Thomas Müntzer's First Publication," SCJ 17 (1986): 455–58. Based on version B.

Müntzer began the letter by bemoaning the fact that few Christians are willing to endure the internal cleansing of their spirit in order to receive the pure Spirit of God:

> It is a great foolishness when many of the elected friends of God think that God should cure Christianity with haste, and help quickly, even though no one longs for it or is at all eager to become poor in spirit by suffering and perseverance (Matthew 5, Luke 6). Whoever does not seek the poverty of his spirit is not worthy of being ruled by God.[26]

He declares that this is the experience to which Psalm 93 refers when it tells of how God first sent the flood of purification and then established eternal reign:

> Before a man can become certain of his salvation, many waves of water will come with a gruesome roar, so that he will lose all desire to stay alive. . . . That is why one should not flee from these waves but rather break them with great skill, just as well-trained sailors do. For the Lord does not want to give someone His holy witness unless he has first worked through his amazement *(Verwunderung)*. That is why human hearts so rarely receive the true Spirit of Christ, who is the owner of souls, that they might have a foretaste of eternal life.[27]

However, when Christians yield to such spiritual suffering, forswearing the dead letter and turning instead to the living Word of God as it erupts in their hearts, they will become "an assembly of the elect" which cannot be overcome by any "charge of gunpowder."[28]

> I hear that you are quite boastful and do not study; that you are negligent; that you talk much about your cause when you are drinking. But [I hear] that when you are sober, you are cowards and afraid. Improve your lives, brethren. Beware of gluttony, Luke 21[:34], 1 Pet. 5[:8]. Flee the passions and the lovers of passions, 2 Tim. 3 [2:22]. Be braver than you were, and write to me how prolific you have been with your talents [Luke 19:12–27].[29]

Back in Allstedt, Müntzer's sermons about a final reformation

26. MSB 22:19–24.
27. MSB 21—22:2, 22:4–9.
28. MSB 23:31–32.
29. MSB 24:17–24.

of the church impressed the simple country folk but angered
Ernest, the Count of Mansfeld and a staunch Catholic. He prohibited his subjects from attending St. John's Church, justifying
his ban on the basis of an imperial edict promulgated on March
6, 1523, which instructed German princes to prohibit any ecclesiastical reform until the convening of another imperial diet.
Elector Frederick the Wise had made it known that he too would
abide by this edict. Thus since Luther's own prince, as well as
the Catholic authorities, had agreed to abide by the edict, both
Catholics and "Protestants" could easily accuse Müntzer of violating imperial law.

When Müntzer heard of Count Ernest's interference in Allstedt
affairs, he decided to preach about it. On September 13, 1523, he
challenged the count from the pulpit, inviting him to appear
before an ecclesiastical tribunal in Allstedt and prove that
Müntzer taught errors and heresies. Müntzer would regard him
as a mischievous knave who deserved no more attention than a
Turk or a heathen if he refused to come. The count's response was
immediate: he sent an official protest to the town council of
Allstedt demanding that Müntzer be arrested.

The town council replied equally quickly. They wrote back
that they had seriously considered Count Ernest's complaint but
they could not arrest Müntzer since the Word of God rather than
criminality was involved. They included letters from both Simon Haferitz and Müntzer.[30]

Haferitz confined himself to a declaration of solidarity with
Müntzer, but Müntzer's letter disclosed an arrogant self-confidence and a conviction of prophetic mission. He did address the
count in traditional polite fashion, but went on to accuse him of
being too hard on his subjects, and vowed to accuse him publicly, since he banned the Gospel, of being no better than a Turk,
a Jew, or a heathen.[31]

> And you should know that in such mighty and just matters I am not
> afraid of the entire world. Christ cries murder concerning those
> who take away the key to God's knowledge. The key to this knowl-

30. The correspondence is contained in Carl E. Förstemann, ed., *Neues Urkundenbuch zur Geschichte der evangelischen Kirchenreformation* (Hamburg:
Perthes, 1842), 228–33. See also E, 383–85.

31. Letter dated September 22, 1523. MSB 394:1–12.

edge is ruling people in such a way that they learn to fear God alone, Romans 13. For the beginning of true Christian wisdom is fear of the Lord. But you want to be feared more than God [is feared], as I shall demonstrate through your doings and your directive. Thus you are the one who takes away the key to the knowledge of God and forbids people to go to church.[32]

Müntzer then repeated what he had already stated in Prague, namely, that he would demonstrate his position on the basis of Scripture and would willingly sacrifice life and limb if he failed; in any event, he would continue the struggle until the end:

> I am a servant of God just as you are. So, since the entire world must be patient, calm down. Don't struggle, or your old coat will tear. If you put pressure on me, I shall deal with you in ways a thousand times worse than Luther used on the pope. If you can bear to, be a gracious lord, and show it. If not, I leave it to God's will. Amen.

He signed the letter, "a destroyer of the unbelievers."[33]

Ernest of Mansfeld sent this letter, together with all the other correspondence between himself and Allstedt, to Elector Frederick and demanded Müntzer's arrest so that his own honor might be restored. He added that he had no choice but to enforce the imperial edict if political unrest were to be avoided.[34] The elector responded, concurring that public slander of government officials should not be tolerated but adding that he would have to investigate this matter further, since he did not know the exact circumstances or the pastor involved; and that he would meanwhile leave the responsibility for further action to the count.[35]

On September 28, 1523, Elector Frederick requested his representative Hans Zeiss and the town council of Allstedt to report to him on the events, and to include their rationale for employing Müntzer. He also demanded they have all pastors refrain from the kind of attacks Müntzer had launched against Ernest of

---

32. MSB 394:12–20.
33. MSB 394:29–36.
34. Förstemann, *Neues Urkundenbuch*, 230–31.
35. Ibid., 232.

Mansfeld.[36] Müntzer promised, by way of a ceremonial handshake at a subsequent town council meeting, to maintain silence until the matter had been dealt with in an appropriate manner, such as a special hearing. He also wrote to Elector Frederick on October 4, 1523, to explain his position. His self-confidence and prophetic strain are once again obvious:

> Most gracious Lord: Since the almighty God made me a true preacher, I have become accustomed to blowing the loud and impelling trumpets so that they blare out with zeal the knowledge of God and do not spare any human being on this earth who resists the word of God, as God Himself commanded through the prophet Isaiah 58[:1]. That is why, (as is only fair) my name must of necessity sound gruesomely ugly and unqualified to those who are worldly clever, Matt. 5[:11], Luke 6[:22]. To lascivious people it is a miserable abomination and swift destruction, but to the poor and needy little community it is a sweet smell of life, 2 Cor. 2[:15–16].[37]

Müntzer then portrayed himself as the prophet who, like Jeremiah or Ezekiel, must save Christianity by proclaiming the true Word of God manifested in the crucified Christ. Count Ernest of Mansfeld had, however, forbidden his people to hear this proclamation, whereupon he, Müntzer, had "miserably exhorted *(erbärmlich vermahnt)*" and invited him to demonstrate the heresy in the proclamation. But instead of asking experts for instruction and advice, the count had used the authority of the imperial edict; such an act only confuses the common people, so that they would end up fearing their princes more than loving them:[38]

> In that case the world will be taken from them and will be given to the fervent people to destroy the ungodly, Dan. 7[:18]. Then that precious treasure, peace, will disappear from the earth, Rev. 6[:2]: the rider on the white horse will conquer, which ought not to happen. Oh noble, gracious Elector, we must be diligent so that our Saviour, on the right hand of God (when He Himself will tend the sheep and drive away the wild animals from the flock) will not shatter the kings on the day of His wrath, Psalm 109 [110:5], Ezek.

36. Ibid., 231. The electoral official Zeiss supported Müntzer in Allstedt. See Wieland Held, "Der Allstedter Schösser Hans Zeiss und sein Verhältnis zu Thomas Müntzer," ZGW 35 (1987): 1073–91.

37. MSB 395:8–17.

38. MSB 395:17—396:26.

34 [:10]. Oh, may this not happen because of our neglect! May God be pleased.[39]

Müntzer asked the elector for a fair hearing, and reminded him that he, Müntzer, was forced to take a stand for God, who had continuously protected him and His people; he signed the letter "a servant of God."[40]

On October 11, 1523, Elector Frederick wrote to Count Ernest telling him that Müntzer had promised to remain silent, but he did not mention Müntzer's letter.[41] The exchange of letters between the Allstedt town council, Count Ernest of Mansfeld, and Elector Frederick had given Müntzer the idea that his prince would leave matters as they were until he received more information. Luther had also expressed a desire to learn more about Müntzer's teaching, and had written to his friend George Spalatin asking him to urge Müntzer to come to Wittenberg for an exchange of ideas.[42]

Müntzer decided to publish an account of his teachings concerning faith, and composed a German treatise entitled *Protest or Presentation of Thomas Müntzer of Stolberg at the Harz, Pastor in Allstedt. Concerning His Teaching About the Origins of the True Christian Faith and About Baptism.* It was published at the beginning of 1524.[43]

Elector Frederick and an entourage that included George Spalatin stayed at the Allstedt castle from November 4 to November 14, 1523, and it is possible that Spalatin may have met with Müntzer. Luther's friend John Lang was also at the Allstedt castle at that time to participate in a dialogue with the Allstedt preachers. However, there is no record of a meeting, except

39. MSB 396:27—397:9.

40. MSB 397:10–19.

41. Förstemann, *Neues Urkundenbuch*, 234.

42. Letter dated August 3, 1523. WA. BR 3:120.34–35.

43. *Protestation oder Entbietung Thomas Müntzer* MSB 225—40. It is possible that this treatise was meant to be Müntzer's position paper to be presented at his pending meeting with Spalatin in Allstedt. The two conclusions (sections 21 and 22) tend to confirm this view. See Siegfried Bräuer, "Die Vorgeschichte von Luthers 'Ein Brief an die Fürsten von Sachsen von dem aufrührerischem Geist,' " LJ 47 (1980): 49–50.

for eleven questions in Spalatin's handwriting concerning
Müntzer's views on faith:[44]

1. What is true Christian faith, and of what does it consist?
2. How does faith originate?
3. Whence is faith to be asked for and sought?
4. How can faith be obtained?
5. How may we usefully and wholesomely teach faith?
6. How may we be certain of our faith?
7. How can and should one prove one's faith?
8. Who are the true faithful Christians?
9. In which temptations does faith originate, in which is it
   sown and increased?
10. How does faith stand up to temptations and emerge vic-
    torious?
11. What is faith, and how does it save?

On the basis of these questions, Spalatin must have been aware
of Müntzer's quest for the origins and the certainty of faith, and
may even have read the *Prague Manifesto* of 1521. Müntzer composed another German treatise entitled *Concerning the Simulated Faith* to answer these questions.[45] It was also published in
1524 as a companion piece to the *Protest*.[46]

The preface to the *Protest* heralds a "happy new year 1524,"
and continues: "Listen world! I preach to you Jesus the crucified
at the new year, and you and I with him. If you like it, receive it;
if you don't like it, reject it."[47] Müntzer then repeats his com-
plaints about the lack of true Christians born again by way of
the Holy Spirit's purification. He declared that the postapostolic
church had become a prostitute by selling out to "a honey-sweet

44. The questions are preserved in MSB 569. Spalatin mentioned "interroga-
tions" *(interrogationes)*. See Irmgard Höss, *Georg Spalatin 1484–1545. Ein Leben
in der Zeit des Humanismus und der Reformation* (Weimar: Böhlard, 1956), 265.
Bräuer ("Die Vorgeschichte," 48, n. 36) discovered the presence of Lang while
researching the semiannual budget of the Allstedt city council. He presents good
arguments in favor of a meeting between Müntzer and Spalatin (ibid.). E, 403
speculates that they did not meet.

45. *Von dem gedichteten Glauben*. MSB 218—24. Müntzer sent the manuscript
to the electoral commissioner Hans Zeiss with a cover letter dated December 2,
1523. MSB 397—98. It is not known whether Zeiss gave the manuscript to
Spalatin, but E, 404–5 thinks it was done.

46. Indicated in the subtitle "issued next to the *Protest*" *(auf nächst Protestation ausgegangen)*. MSB 218:1.

47. MSB 225.

Jesus;" that it existed without suffering, without the Holy Spirit, and that its leaders were scribes who introduced the external monkey-business of the cult of saint, the invocation of Mary, and infant baptism:

> True baptism has been misunderstood. That is why entering Christianity has become a beastly monkey-business. Using a foundation of sand, the scribes have betrayed miserable, sad, dear Christianity beyond measure.[48]

According to Müntzer, the prostitute church and its scribes ignored the biblical link between faith and baptism as stated in the Gospel of John: like Nicodemus, one must be born again through the Holy Spirit before one is baptized (John 3:5). Whenever Jesus spoke of "thirst" and "water," he meant the internal, purifying flow of the Holy Spirit in the human heart. This experience of rebirth is like a sharp plowshare exposing sinful creatureliness and preparing for the advent of God's Spirit in the depth of one's soul.

Müntzer also attacked those who, like Luther, speak of becoming righteous by faith alone rather than by good works. "This is misleading talk," because it presumed that there is no human work involved in the process of salvation, he claimed. "But one must describe how it feels to be poor in spirit and confirm it through the blessed fathers and Scripture."[49] Faith does not come by believing what is written and said by other people but by an intensive, independent, and personal awareness that God has begun a struggle against one's own nature.

> It is the diligent waiting for the Word that makes a beginning Christian. During this waiting one must first suffer the Word, and there must not be any consolation in the fact that our works are delayed. Then one thinks one has no faith at all; indeed, one feels that no faith will come. There is a meager desire for true faith, but it is so weak that one is hardly aware of it. Finally, one must break down and lament, "Oh what a miserable man I am! What drives me in my heart? My conscience eats up all my strength and everything I am. What shall I do? I have lost confidence in God."[50]

It is this state of utter despair that Müntzer regards as the

48. MSB 228:13–16.
49. MSB 235:30—236:4.
50. MSB 237:21–31.

beginning of faith. But, he avers, the established church does not want to acknowledge such internal suffering as God's work. Its scribes counsel:

"Well, my dear fellow, you should not become preoccupied with such high matters. Simply believe, and don't think about it. It is pure fantasy. Join the people and be merry! Then you will forget your trouble." You see, dear brother, this kind of consolation has made an abomination out of all Christian seriousness.[51]

He concluded the treatise by presenting himself as the reformer who would do more for the universal church than all the others:

I shall direct the teaching of the evangelical preachers in a better fashion through my undertaking, as well as not neglecting our backward slow Roman brethren. Just place my judgment before the whole world. Don't put it into a corner. I stake my life on it, with no deceitful defense.[52]

In *Concerning the Simulated Faith*, Müntzer dealt with the question of faith in fourteen brief segments. He began with the definition: "Christian faith is a safeguard *(Sicherung)*, to rely on the word and promise of Christ."[53] This Word and promise are cruciform—they penetrate into the heart of the patiently waiting Christians and make them "diligent disciples" of their master. One remains a simulated believer unless one can give an account of this experience of conversion.[54] The models of true faith are Abraham, Moses, and Stephen, for they came to know the original unity between God and God's creatures. The Bible demonstrates how one must suffer before one receives the living Word of God.

We who are not tempted have such high regard for ourselves that we improvise with a simulated faith and with a simulated mercy of God; we trust a natural promise or assurance and wish to use them to storm heaven. Oh no, dearest Christians! Let us use the holy Bible for what it was made to be, to kill, not to create life, as the living word that a soul hears does. Let us not take a piece from here and another piece from there. It is in the teaching of the spirit and

51. MSB 238:15–20.
52. MSB 240:2–6.
53. MSB 218:5–6.
54. MSB 218:6–25.

not of the flesh that we should put together what needs to be attended to everywhere in Scripture so that it may console and terrify.[55]

A preacher like John the Baptist, who cried in the wilderness and announced the advent of the living word, is needed to overcome simulated faith.[56] At issue is conformity to the crucified Christ: "Whoever refuses the bitter Christ will gorge himself to death on honey."[57] Müntzer uses mystical terms to describe this cruciformity:

> Whoever looks in such a manner towards the little lamb that takes away the sin of the world will say, "With my own ears have I heard how the ancient fathers in the Bible dealt with God and how God dealt with them. None became one with Him until they overcame through suffering [eternally appropriate for them]. To move from light to light is the result of God's illumination."[58]

Mystical experience is, for Müntzer, the true foundation of Christianity and the leaven that the new scribes have tried to transform into a simulated faith.

Müntzer's polemics against the "simulated faith" of the existing church encouraged some of his adherents to take action against the false church of the ungodly. On March 24, 1524, Maundy Thursday, they burned down the small Mallerbach chapel outside of Allstedt. No one was injured, but the deed was done because Müntzer had declared the chapel a house of idolatry where the Virgin Mary was being worshiped and false claims of her miraculous powers were attracting superstitious people. Müntzer probably did not himself participate in the event.[59] The Mallerbach affair was linked to an organization consisting of about thirty people who had formed a "league" *(Bund)* sometime earlier. When or how the league originated is unknown, but

55. MSB 220:19–28.
56. MSB 221:23—222:5.
57. MSB 222:22–23.
58. MSB 223:10–15.

59. In 1525 he confessed that "he had been there" and then described how the chapel had been destroyed. MSB 556:11–16. E, 419 speculates that Müntzer might have witnessed the event without participating. Bensing *(Thomas Müntzer,* 56) claims Müntzer defended the action in his sermons. In any event, Müntzer did encourage and defend this kind of action.

its aims, later disclosed by members who were apprehended in connection with the peasants' rebellion in 1525, were: "to stand by the Gospel, to refuse to pay taxes to monks and nuns, and to assist in driving them out and to destroy them."[60] The legal owner of the Mallerbach chapel, the abbess of the nunnery in Naundorf, immediately complained to Duke John of Saxony who had already heard rumors of possible unrest in Allstedt.[61] Fearing reprisals from outsiders, many citizens joined the league.

Duke John ordered the electoral commissioner, the mayor of Allstedt, and the town council to appear before him for a hearing in Weimar on May 9, 1524. At the hearing, he gave them fourteen days to find and to punish the persons who had participated in the Mallerbach affair. The Allstedt authorities promised to obey, but were apparently convinced that too much was being made of the whole affair; after all, both Duke John and Elector Frederick favored the reform movement, and their preachers Müntzer and Haferitz were doing their best to aid the reform. Indeed, twenty days later, on May 29, 1524, no action had yet been taken, and the electoral commissioner Zeiss pleaded for patience when he reported to Duke John. Zeiss declared that the matter was not important enough to warrant harsh reprisal; and any harsh action of the sort might endanger his own life at the hands of the Allstedt citizens.[62] However, on June 4, 1524, the electoral commissioner had a member of the town council

60. Quoted in the protocol of June 10, 1525, during questioning of league members. See Carl E. Förstemann, "Zur Geschichte des Bauernkrieges im Thüringischen und Mansfeldischen," *Neue Mitteilungen aus dem Gebiet historischer-antiquarischer Forschungen* 12 (1869): 215. Hinrichs (*Luther und Müntzer*, 12) assumes that the league had been formed shortly before the attack on the Mallerbach chapel. Bräuer ("Thomas Müntzer und der Allstedter Bund," 88) argues that the league originated in the summer of 1523 and was then expanded in June 1524. There is unconvincing evidence in Carl Hinrichs, *Luther und Müntzer. Ihre Auseinandersetzung über Obrigkeit und Widerstandsrecht*, Arbeiten zur Kirchengeschichte 29 (Berlin: Walter de Gruyter, 1962), 18. See also Manfred Bensing, "Idee und Praxis des 'christlichen Verbündnisses' bei Thomas Müntzer" in Abraham Friesen and Hans-Jürgen Goertz, eds., *Thomas Müntzer*, Wege der Forschung, no. 491 (Darmstadt: Wissenschaftliche Buchgesellschaft, 1978), 307. E, 430–31 leaves the question of origins open due to a lack of clear evidence.

61. When Frederick the Wise became elector of Saxony in 1486 and resided in Wittenberg, he made his brother John co-regent to reside in Weimar, southwest of Wittenberg in Thuringia.

62. Förstemann, "Zur Geschichte des Bauernkrieges," 158.

arrested in order to pacify the duke. The council then sent a letter to Duke John to justify the Mallerbach arson as an act against unjust taxation by ungodly monasteries. They urged the duke not to defend the ungodly, since divine law prohibited it (Exod. 23:1).[63]

The electoral commissioner continued to press the town council to make more arrests, with the help of outsiders if necessary. Many Allstedters objected; Müntzer urged them to arm themselves against outside attacks. On June 13, a large group of armed citizens led by Müntzer's league stood all night in a vigil until the commissioner capitulated and arranged the release of the one town council member so far arrested. Elector Frederick finally entered the dispute personally, and on June 27, 1524, ordered the town council to move swiftly against all offenders. As far as the Allstedt preachers were concerned, they were to have a hearing to determine whether or not their preaching was of God—a reference to the wise counsel of Gamaliel in Acts 5:38.[64]

Müntzer and his adherents considered this attitude to be a license to proceed with their plans to transform Allstedt into a base for actions against the ungodly. The league was expanded to include outsiders from surrounding villages and towns, and military exercises were held. The lines were now drawn.

63. Letter dated June 7, 1524. MSB 405:20–24.
64. Förstemann, "Zur Geschichte des Bauernkrieges," 168.

5

THE NEW DANIEL

By the summer of 1524, political attention in Saxony was focused on Müntzer and Allstedt. Luther had urged the Saxon
princes to bring Müntzer to Wittenberg for a hearing of his
views. But when Müntzer had instead begun to publish treatises
in Allstedt, Luther was quick to label him "satanic" because he
refused to have his "spirit examined and instead remained in his
own corner."[1]

The princes decided to see personally what was going on in
Allstedt. Duke John of Saxony ordered Müntzer to prepare a
sermon to be presented before the princes on July 13, 1524, since
they planned to stop at the Allstedt castle on their journey from
Weimar to Halberstadt on that day. Attending the sermon presentation that morning were Duke John, his son the crown
prince John Frederick, electoral chancellor George Brück, court
councilor Hans of Grefendorf, and a small group of courtiers.[2]

Müntzer decided to present an exposition of Daniel 2, the
passage in which Daniel interprets the king's dreams to the
Babylonian king Nebuchadnezzar; he entitled his sermon *An
Exposition of the Prophet Daniel's Discernment.*[3] He began with a

---

1. In a letter dated June 18, 1524, to Crown Prince John Frederick. WA.BR
3:307. 69.

2. Hinrichs (*Luther und Müntzer,* 39) and Bensing (*Thomas Müntzer,* 56) assume, albeit without evidence, that the mayor and members of the town council
were also present. E, 443 does not. See Förstemann, "Zur Geschichte des
Bauernkrieges," 188.

3. *Auslegung des anderen Unterschieds Danielis . . .*, MSB 242—263. The word
"Unterschied" means "critical distinction"; thus the translation "discernment."

lamentation about the state of Christianity, stating that hardly anyone cared any longer about the biblical admonitions to submit themselves to purification from sin so as to be ready to receive the Spirit of God in order to be faithful witnesses in a dangerous world. He quoted passage after passage from Scripture and referred to his study of ancient Christian history to make his point:

> Thus I say that the original church has become ramshackle in all places, up to the time of the separated world, Luke 21 [2:10], Dan. 2[:35], Ezra 4. In the fourth book, chapter 22, Hegesippus and Eusebius say about the Christian church that the Christian community remained a virgin only until the death of the apostles' disciples. Soon thereafter it became an adulteress, as the dear apostles had prophesied 2 Pet. 2[:14].[4]

Müntzer supported this argument with various citations from Scripture, focusing on the prophecy that Christ the rock (1 Cor. 10:4) would be rejected—first at the time of his birth, and again at the present time.[5] He suggested a reason for this:

> They [the generations following the apostles' disciples] have rejected the true knowledge of God and substituted for it a nice, fine, golden god on which the poor peasants feed, as Hosea clearly says in chapter 4[:8] and Lamentations confirms [4:5]. "Those who feasted on dainties have now received dirt and mire." Oh, the deplorable miserable abomination, of which Christ Himself speaks in Matt. 24[:15]! He is being so terribly slandered by the devilish Mass, by ungodly preaching and ungodly style of life! The result still remains nothing but a wooden god.[6]

That is the reason, Müntzer asserted, why Jews and heathen have no respect for Christianity and why Christ has become a mere spectacle, somewhat like an annual fair; and he urged:

> Therefore, my dear brethren, we must rise from this filth and become true disciples of God taught by God, John 6[:48], Matt. 23[:8–10]. We shall need tremendous power—which will be granted from above—to punish this unspeakable wickedness and to destroy it. That [power] is the clearest knowledge of God (Prov.

4. MSB 243:20—244:4.
5. MSB 244:5–28.
6. MSB 245:10–19.

9[:10]) born solely out of pure true fear of God. It alone must arm us with the greatest zeal to retaliate against the enemies of God, as is written in Prov. 5[:18], John 2[:17], Psalm 68 [69:10]. There can be no excuse, no human or rational intentions, for the ungodly are as immeasurably beautiful and cunning as the beautiful cornflower growing among the ears of wheat (Eccles. 8[:14]). Those who have wisdom about God must know this.[7]

Such wisdom, Müntzer declared, is received directly from God, refuting the teaching of the church scribes who claim that God no longer grants power through visions or the immediate, living Word. They, like the religious leaders at the time of King Nebuchadnezzar, say that God no longer speaks directly to his people; and they poke fun at those who make such claims. But Daniel (2:47) testifies that even the heathen Nebuchadnezzar accepted the directly imparted divine prophecy in his dreams.[8]

Müntzer then began his exposition of Dan. 2:1–13: the statements about the king's false prophets and magicians point to the religious leaders of Müntzer's own time; they too talk a lot about faith yet are unable to demonstrate its power. These scribes do not see the harmony of the Old with the New Testament regarding the revelation of God's Spirit (Daniel 2; Isa. 64:3; 1 Cor. 2:9), namely, that it comes through the believers' inner turmoil and suffering, which purifies them from creaturely selfishness. The existence of this harmony is essential in Müntzer's view:

> That is why St. Paul cites Moses and Isaiah in Rom. 10[:8, 20, Deut. 30:14, and Isa. 65:1] and there speaks of how the inner word is heard, through the revelation of God, in the depth of the soul. Whoever has not become aware and receptive to this living witness of God (Rom. 8[:2]) could not say anything substantial about God, even if he had swallowed a hundred thousand Bibles.[9]

He constantly stressed one's need to endure inner turmoil before the Holy Spirit could liberate the soul from the bondage of creatureliness. Visions play a decisive role in this process, just as they did in the experience of Nebuchadnezzar.

> The elect must pay attention to the work of visions to make sure

7. MSB 246:4–16.
8. MSB 246:23—247:1, 18–33.
9. MSB 251:14–19.

that they are not the result of human intentions but issue forth simply according to God's immovable will. One must be very cautious not to miss an iota of what one has seen, so that its work can be done well.[10]

Müntzer told the princes that Scripture and human experience warn against the devil who, working in many disguises, falsifies visions, but that visions nevertheless have a decisive place in God's economy of salvation. Without referring to anyone by name, he attacked those who, like "brother fattened pig" (Mastschwein) and "soft-living brother" (Sanftleben), reject visions. He insisted that "one must have visions if one has not noticed God's clear Word in one's soul."[11] To prove his point, he cited the vision that got St. Paul out of jail (Acts 12:7).[12]

> What is the purpose of the biblical texts about visions? It is indeed true that the spirit of God now reveals to many pious and chosen people the great necessity for a decisive, invincible reformation in the future, and this must come to pass. No matter who is against it, the prophecy of Daniel stands fast even if no one wants to believe it, as Paul also says in Rom. 3[:3]. This text of Daniel's is as clear as the sun, and the end of the fifth empire is in full swing now.[13]

Müntzer equated his era with the fifth empire in Daniel's text. It is a mixture of iron (the attempt to use force) and clay (the filth existing in the church). He thus rejected the medieval combination of church and state known as the Holy Roman Empire. According to Müntzer, the first empire was that of the Babylonians, the second was that of the Medes and the Persians, the third was that of the Greeks, and the fourth was that of the Romans, and this final fifth empire is that of the Holy Roman Empire. The history of the five empires is a story of decline, but a final opportunity to set things right does exist. And he counseled:

> Therefore, my dearest regents, attain your knowledge directly from the mouth of God and do not be seduced by your hypocritical priests who restrain you with their false talk about God's goodness

10. MSB 253:6–11.
11. MSB 254:12–14.
12. MSB 254:22–26, 255:5–10.
13. MSB 255:22–30.

and patience. The rock torn from the mountain without the use of hands [Dan. 2:34] has become large. The poor lay people and peasants have focused on it better than you have. Indeed, God be praised, it has become so large that other lords or neighbors would be driven off by their own people if they wanted to persecute you for defending the gospel. That I know for sure.[14]

By using "rock" and "mountain," Müntzer was trying to woo the princes away from Luther and Rome into his own camp. He explained that his was a community of people chosen by God to undertake the final reformation before Christ's second coming. Christ was the rock that became a new mountain, from which the Holy Spirit was proceeding to do God's final bidding. He exhorted:

> Therefore, my dear regents of Saxony, step confidently on the cornerstone [Christ] just as St. Peter did (Matt. 16[:18]) and seek the true steadfastness that the divine will bestows. It will safeguard you well on the stone (Psalm 39 [40:3]). Your path will be the right one. Just seek God's justice and join the cause of the Gospel. God is nearer to you than you believe.[15]

Müntzer then moved to the main point of his sermon, the need for a new Daniel in that time of crisis caused by the prostitution of the church:

> That is why a new Daniel must appear and interpret for you your revelation; and he must lead the way, as Moses teaches, Deut. 20[:2]. He must placate the wrath of the princes and that of the furious people. For when you truly experience the damage to Christendom and the deception of the false priests and desperate villains, you too will become furious at them beyond anyone's imagination. You will have doubts and become well aware that you have been so gracious after they have led you to make the most disgraceful judgments with the sweetest words, Prov. 6[:1–5] against all established truth.[16]

Müntzer told the princes that he disagreed with Luther's declaration that government was instituted by God and was based on Rom. 13:1. He urged them to reject that notion and instead to

14. MSB 256:17–24.
15. MSB 256:29—257:6.
16. MSB 257:19–29.

heed the words of Christ, who proclaimed that the sword should
be used to create a theocracy, with the words "I have not come to
bring peace but the sword" (Matt. 10:34).

> What shall one do with it [the sword]? Nothing else than removing
> and separating the evil ones who impede the Gospel, for otherwise
> you are not the servants of God that Paul calls you in Rom. 13[:4].
> You should not despair. God will smash all the opponents who dare
> to persecute you, for His hand has not yet grown smaller, as Isa.
> 59[:1] says. Therefore He still wishes to help you, and will do so,
> just as He stood by Josiah the chosen King [2 Kings 22—23] and by
> the others who defended His name. Thus, as Peter says (2 Pet. 1[:4]),
> you are angels when you intend to do right. Christ commanded
> with great seriousness (Luke 19[:27]), "But as for these enemies of
> mine who did not want me to reign over them, bring them here and
> slay them in front of me."[17]

According to Müntzer, the biblical God calls for a theocracy—
divine rule by the sword—to protect God's law fulfilled in
Christ. For that reason the princes should understand their
mission to be the removal of God's enemies, which is why God
had given them the sword. Daniel had become the official
(Amtmann) whose duty it was to make certain that God's will
was done, and Müntzer gave clear instructions as to what must
be done:

> If you wish to be true regents, you must begin your reign at the
> roots, as Christ commanded: you must drive His enemies from
> among the elect, because you are the means with which to do it.
> Dear ones, do not offer the excuse that the power of God should do
> it without the aid of your sword, for your sword may rust in its
> sheath. . . . Therefore, do not let the evildoers, who turn away from
> God, live (Deut. 13[:6]). If the ungodly impede the pious, they no
> longer have the right to live; in Exod. 22[:2], God says, "Do not let
> the evildoers live." St. Paul in Rom. 13[:4] means the same thing
> when he says of the sword of regents that it is given to punish the
> evil and protect the pious.[18]

He concluded the sermon by stating that, like Nebuchadnezzar,
the princes should accept the wisdom of Daniel, meaning
Müntzer, and that they should join those already touched by the

17. MSB 258:3–15.
18. MSB 259:1–6, 13–19.

Holy Spirit, for they represented the new community to come after the demise of the five empires.

The ungodly have no right to live unless the elect permit it, as is written in Exod. 23[:29–33]. Rejoice, true friends of God, that the hearts of the enemies of the cross have fallen into their boots. They must do right even though they never dreamed of doing so. If we fear God, why should we be afraid of loose and unfit people? (Num. 14[:8–9], Josh. 11[:6]). Be of good cheer! He to whom all power in heaven and on earth is given intends to reign Himself (Matt. 28[:18]).[19]

Müntzer continued to advocate his cause, although the princes' reaction to his sermon is not known. He wrote a letter to Duke John on the same day he preached that sermon, to declare that not just Wittenberg but the whole world must judge him.

I shall not shun the light. I want to be interrogated, because of the horrible offence against the elect. But I will not agree if you wish me to be interrogated only in Wittenberg. I want Romans, Turks and heathen involved, for I am addressing all of foolish Christendom and totally rebuking it. I am prepared to give a responsible account of my faith.[20]

He offered all his writings for the duke's inspection, since they might remind the duke of divine revelation and thus justify Müntzer.[21]

On July 15, 1524, Müntzer wrote letters to the "God-fearing and persecuted Christians" of Sangerhausen and to the Sangerhausen town council. To his supporters he wrote:

If you truly fear God, this must result in your confronting the fearful danger on earth caused by the impertinence of the ungodly's fleshly minds. God's goodness should move you in this direction. There is now such a rich supply of it that more than thirty leagues of the elect have been created thus far. The game is afoot everywhere.[22]

The second letter warned the town council not to interfere with

19. MSB 262:32—263:7. Bensing (*Thomas Müntzer*, 59) speculates that the sermon foreshadows class struggles as taken up by Marxism.
20. MSB 407:20–25.
21. MSB 407:27–30.
22. MSB 408:18–23. There are no good reasons to change the date, as E, 474 suggests. The two letters are in MSB 408—9, and MSB 411—15.

the Word of God. If they did so, he would unleash his disciples against them.

> You want to prohibit the word of God and yet be Christians? Oh, how well that is reconciled! I swear that if you do not improve in this matter, I shall no longer hold back the people who can molest you. You must choose: either accept the Gospel, or expose yourselves before the heathen. The latter is harder [to do] than iron is strong. I shall complain to the entire world that you are the meatfly that soils the ointment of the Holy Spirit.[23]

Müntzer's attempt to win over his friend Carlstadt failed. Carlstadt and his congregation in Orlamünde told Müntzer in no uncertain terms that true faith and violence do not mix.[24] But Müntzer's passionate preaching did have its effect, and he succeeded in winning support from people in many villages and towns near Allstedt. When on July 24, 1524, he preached about the divinely willed league of the elect, explicating the story of God's covenant with King Josiah (2 Kings 22—23), there were about three hundred people present, and the Allstedt town council joined Müntzer's league of the elect.[25]

As a result, Müntzer wrote to the electoral commissioner Hans Zeiss to urge him not to oppose the new movement. He declared that he had no objections to the rule of princes, as long as they adhered to the true Christian faith—that is, as long as they experienced the purification of their souls and received the Holy Spirit. But, he added, the most recent events in and around Allstedt suggested that they not only resisted faith but also violated natural law by persecuting decent Christians who had come as refugees to Allstedt. "Since they not only act against the faith but also against natural law, one should strangle them like dogs."[26] He hoped Zeiss would understand that what was happening was but a part of a large movement disclosing the rela-

---

23. MSB 410:22–29.

24. Letter to Müntzer written sometime in July 1524. MSB 571:8–10. The Orlamünde treatise to the Allstedter on *How One Should Fight in a Christian Way (Wie man christlich fechten soll)* has been reprinted in Adolf Laube et al., eds., *Flugschriften der frühen Reformationsbewegung 1518–1524*, 2 vols. (Berlin: Akademieverlag; Vaduz: Topos, 1982), 1:443–45.

25. Müntzer mentions the sermon in a letter to Hans Zeiss on July 25, 1524. MSB 421:3–10.

26. MSB 417:11–13. Letter dated July 22, 1524.

tionship between God and his creatures; the time had come when the creatures who had once been part of God must be reunited with God, like parts to the whole.

The will of God is the totality of all its parts. To recognize the knowledge and judgment of God is the explanation of this same will, as Paul writes in Col. 1[:9], Psalm 118. But the work of God flows from the whole into all its parts.[27]

In another letter to Zeiss, he described the mystical unity existing between God and his creatures which, after the fall of Adam and Eve, must be recaptured through the creature's spiritual transformation. He added that he had described this transformation in his treatise *Concerning the Simulated Faith* as the experiencing of the Holy Spirit in the depth of the soul.[28] Müntzer explained that since the ungodly, many princes among them, had rejected this transformation and had even persecuted those who had experienced it, the "league of the elect" had been formed as a means of self-defense that should not be denied to true Christians.[29] "If the elect would simply submit to martyrdom, the knavery of the ungodly would not be discovered at all, and God's witness would have no chance to succeed."[30] He advised Zeiss that for that reason he should be careful in considering the sources of his information and counsel.

On July 28, 1524, Zeiss submitted a report to Duke John in Weimar, in which he stressed the necessity of listening to Müntzer before determining what should be done in Allstedt. Echoing Elector Frederick the Wise, he recommended that Duke John first ascertain whether or not the matter was of God; if it were of God, one should not interfere.[31] The response from Weimar was a command to hold a hearing on the Allstedt situation, with a special session devoted to Müntzer.

This hearing was influenced at the outset by the publication of Luther's attack on Müntzer, *Letter to the Princes of Saxony Con-*

27. MSB 418:23–26.

28. MSB 418:19. Müntzer did not mention the title of the treatise, but it was enclosed in the letter to Zeiss. MSB 217.

29. Letter dated July 25, 1524. MSB 423:5–7.

30. MSB 423:19–22.

31. Text of the report in Förstemann, "Zur Geschichte des Bauernkrieges," 179–82.

cerning the Rebellious Spirit.[32] In his attack, Luther conceded that the Word of God should have free reign, but he advised the princes to intervene when preachers like Müntzer "begin to destroy and use force"; at this point they should be banished from the country.[33] Müntzer was the first to be interrogated, and was indeed the focus of the hearing. At issue was his instigation of paramilitary leagues which had disturbed the peace. He defended his position, declaring that he would not change his mind until he had been heard before an "impartial Christian assembly."[34] When questioned, the Allstedt mayor and the members of the town council pleaded innocent to the charge of participating in Müntzer's activities, claiming they had been spellbound by his oratory, and promised not to get involved again. The official record of the hearing clearly establishes Müntzer as the villain, in order to provide the elector with good reason to follow Luther's advice and banish Müntzer from the territory.

Müntzer reacted to the climate of suspicion and his sense of having been betrayed by the Allstedters by writing to Elector Frederick on August 3 to explain his position again. It was also his response to what he considered slanderous accusations made by Luther.

> I preach a Christian faith that disagrees with that of Luther. But it is the same as that in the hearts of all the elect on earth (Psalm 67). Even if one were born a Turk, one would have the beginning of this same faith—that is, the movement of the Holy Spirit which was written about Cornelius in Acts 10[:44–47]. Therefore, if I were to be put on trial before Christendom, the people from all nations who have suffered overwhelming turmoil *(Anfechtung)* in their faith and who have endured despair and are constantly reminded of it should be informed, summoned, and assigned to this trial. People like these I would tolerate as judges.[35]

32. WA 15:210–21. LW 40:49–59.

33. WA 15:219, 5–7, LW 40:57. It is difficult to assess what influence the publication of this letter had on the princes. E (496) states that Duke John was greatly influenced by it. Bräuer ("Die Vorgeschichte," 70) disagrees, since Müntzer was not banished.

34. *Vor einer christlichen ungefehrlichen Gemeinde*, Förstemann, "Zur Geschichte des Bauernkrieges," 189. Müntzer may have met the court chaplain Jacob Strauss at this time in Weimar (see his *Confession* of 1525, MSB 545:13–14) but the evidence is too fragmentary for certainty. See E, 498–99.

35. MSB 430:29—431:7.

He pleaded with the elector to listen to grievances of those who had experienced true faith, and added that he, "a servant of God," would submit another summary of his views to Duke John.[36]

What troubled Müntzer most was the betrayal of the All-stedters who had collapsed under fire at the hearing. Sometime on or before August 7, 1524, he abruptly left town in the company of an obscure goldsmith, leaving his wife and child in Allstedt. He went to the city of Mühlhausen, west of Allstedt. Why did he leave so suddenly?

Two letters, dated August 7 and August 15, explain a little but not much of his reasoning. In one letter he told the electoral commissioner and the town council that he had to travel on behalf of his cause, and that he commended them to God.[37] In the other letter, addressed to the people of Allstedt, he declared that he refused to remain silent despite what had been expected of him after the hearing at Weimar.

> What more shall I do? Should I perhaps remain silent like a dumb dog? Then why should I make a living off the altar? I have told you before how one should behave at a time of turmoil. Should I perhaps yield and suffer death just so the ungodly can do their own thing because of my patience and then say they had strangled Satan? Not at *all!* My fear of God will not make room for someone else's insolence.[38]

Yet he was not bitter. He assured them that he loved them despite what had happened, and he admonished them to overcome their problems until the time when the whole church would be agitated by the "fire of scandal" *(Ärgernis)*.[39]

36. MSB 431:32–35.

37. The German is not too clear: *"Ich hab meiner Sac Gelegenheit haben müssen über Land ziehen."* MSB 432:7–8.

38. MSB 435:1–9.

39. MSB 435:33—436:4. Two drafts of letters, dated August 1524, were found among Müntzer's belongings, and bitterly referred to the betrayal of those who were at the hearing in Weimar. MSB 433:6–20.

6

FINAL APPEALS

Before he left Allstedt, Müntzer drafted the summary of his theological position he had promised Elector Frederick.[1] He submitted a shorter version to the Weimar court and had a longer version printed in Nuremberg after his arrival in Mühlhausen. Both drafts are an interpretation of Luke 1, the story of the birth of John the Baptist and his prophecy of Christ's coming.

Müntzer's intention is already evident in the title: *An Explicit Exposure of the False Faith of the Unfaithful World Enunciated In the Testimony of the Gospel of Luke, as a Reminder to Miserable, Wretched Christendom of Its Fall Into Error (Ezekiel 8). Dear Comrades, Let Us Widen the Peephole So that the Whole World May See and Apprehend Who Our Bigwigs [Grosse Hansen] Are Who Have So Slanderously Transformed God Into a Painted Mannequin (Jeremiah 23). Thomas Müntzer With the Hammer.*[2]

Müntzer stated that, like the prophet Jeremiah, he intended to let the world know what God has to say, especially about victory over the ungodly (Jer. 1:9–10, 18–19), since Jeremiah had himself been attacked in slanderous writings (a reference to Luther's attacks on Müntzer). Just as the prophet Ezekiel had once carved

1. MSB 431:32–35.
2. *Ausgedrückte Entblössung des falschen Glaubens der ungetreuen Welt durchs Zeugnis des Evangeliums von Lukas vorgetragen, der elenden, erbärmlichen Christenheit zur Erinerung ihres Irrsals. Ezechiel 8. Liebe Gesellen, lasst uns das Loch weiter machen, auf dass alle Welt sehen und greifen mag, wer unsere grossen Hansen sind, die Gott so lästerlich zum gemalten Männlein gemacht haben. Jeremiah 23, Thomas Müntzer mit dem Hammer.* MSB 267—319. I am quoting the longer version.

a peephole in the wall of the royal court to expose the abomina-
tions occurring inside, so Müntzer would now widen the
peephole to expose the scribes who shunned the living word of
God (Ezek. 8:7), and to let the flood of true faith confront the
mire that was threatening "the friends of God" (Pss. 93:3–4;
69:2). He, Müntzer, would rescue them from this evil mire and
instruct them in the true faith.[3]

Turning to Luke 1, Müntzer deplored the present rarity of
Luke's kind of faith, although Christ himself, as well as Isaiah
and Paul, had prophesied it (Isa. 65:1–2; Luke 1:18; Rom. 10:16,
20–21).

> It is an unspeakable misery and aggravating abomination that
> people without faith (as is quite obvious) want to preach to people
> a Christian faith they themselves have never found or experienced;
> nor do they know how the faithful feel. As they always boast, they
> think that it is easy to gain faith.[4]

But, he continued, the story of Zachariah and Mary in Luke 1
shows how difficult it is to believe promises that seem to be
impossible to achieve (Luke 1:18, 29).

> They did not gain their faith, as the foolish world now believes, in
> an artificial way. They did not rush in saying, "Yes, I simply believe;
> God will cure everything." The world invents a poisoned faith with
> talk about this kind of superficial advent of faith, a faith much
> worse than the faith of Turks, Jews, or heathen. But Mary and
> Zachariah kept their fear of God until the faith of the mustard seed
> overcame their lack of faith; and all this happened with great fear
> and trembling.[5]

Müntzer cited many scriptural passages to show how a person
proceeds from an existential fear of God to the certainty of faith
accomplished by the Holy Spirit's Word in one's heart, and
described this process in mystical terms.

> Whoever believes easily has an easy heart. But fear of God makes
> room for the Holy Spirit, allowing the elect to be overshadowed by
> that which will greatly damage the world in its wisdom, and of
> which, in its foolishness, it is afraid.

3. *Preface to Poor, Confused Christendom (Vorrede an die arme, zerstreute Christenheit).* MSB 267:33—270:28.

4. MSB 271:9–22.

5. MSB 272:1–17.

That is why one must take notice, in the beginning and end of this Gospel [Luke 1], of the overshadowing of the Holy Spirit who teaches us faith by way of pure fear of God. This fear of God brings forth a great wonder at the impossible work of faith when the power of the Most High (as Luke describes it in the beginning and in the end) totally rejects all the simulated faith or secret lack of faith discovered with the advent and breakthrough [of the Holy Spirit] in the depth of the soul.[6]

He went on to state that those scribes who had a simulated faith always spoke of Scripture rather than of the existential experiencing of faith, even though the common people could not read Scripture. The scribes then told people what to believe. Faith came to the true believer by a different route.

Even if one had never heard or seen the Bible in one's lifetime, one could still have an unfailing Christian faith because of the Spirit's true teaching—as did all those who wrote Holy Scripture without the aid of any books. And one could be quite certain that such faith came from the unfailing God and was not derived from the inventions of the devil or from human nature.[7]

Müntzer contended that the Bible does not create, but confirms true faith, for this faith is the result of the experiencing of the Holy Spirit in one's heart. As such, he was opposed to the scribes, who would cry, "Spirit here, Spirit there!" and emphasized only the written word, and who created various traditions or declared things heretical on the basis of their own opinions,[8] thus ignoring the transforming power of the Holy Spirit. Müntzer described this power as that which would truly deify believers, a description used by the ancient Greek church fathers.

[True faith makes it possible] that we fleshly, earthly humans should become gods through the incarnation of Christ and thus become with him God's disciples, taught by him and deified [vergottet], indeed totally transformed [verwandelt], so that earthly life turns toward heaven (Phil. 3[:20–21]).[9]

6. MSB 273:30—274:12. German mystics like Tauler and Eckhart use terms like "overshadowing" (umschatten), "wonder" (Verwunderung), "abyss of the soul" (Abgrund der Seele), "advent and breakthrough" (Antun und Durchgang).

7. MSB 277:25—278:6.

8. MSB 278:37—280:34.

9. MSB 281:22–32.

Müntzer insisted that Luther became agitated about the wrong issue when he attacked those who experienced the beginning of faith when the Holy Spirit overshadowed their hearts.

> Oh why does Brother Soft Life [*Sanftleben*] or Father Pussyfoot [*Leisetritt*] get so excited? (Job 28). He thinks he can show off the pleasures he has adopted, his pomp and his riches, and have a true faith at the same time—something the Son of God criticized in clear words when he told the scribes in John 5[:44], "How can you believe when you seek your own glory?"[10]

Hypocritical scribes and tyrannical princes cooperated in establishing a false faith, Müntzer asserted, but now the time had come to judge them.

> That God has sent His light into the world in our time is proven by the fact that the ungodly and foolish human political authorities rage so much against God and His anointed (Psalm 2, 1 John 2[:16–20]). Some of them, with the help of Christendom, have just begun to persecute, torture and kill both strangers and their subjects, so that even God can no longer bear look at this misery and, for the sake of the elect, must shorten their days (Matt. 24[:22]).[11]

According to Müntzer, Luke 1:52 testified that God deposed the mighty from their thrones because they desired to be the masters of Christian faith. This desire for domination was but the result of creaturely selfishness.

> Because man fell from God to [a place among] the creatures, it is only proper that (to his own detriment) he has to fear creatures more than God. That is why Paul says, in Rom. 13[:3] that princes exist not because of our fear of good works but because of our fear of being executed for doing evil. Thus they are nothing but executioners and bailiffs; that is their only trade.[12]

To Müntzer the church, just like the state, contained an unhealthy mixture of hypocrites and truly faithful people, for it was possible to join the church without having the Holy Spirit.[13] But the time had come, he asserted, for the common people, particularly the poor peasants, to learn the difference between

10. MSB 282:8–21.
11. MSB 282:8–21.
12. MSB 285:4–17.
13. MSB 287:12–17.

true and false faith, even though they may still be under the spell of the scribes and princes who told them not to worry but to trust their lords: "Oh what great miserable blindness! Would that everyone learned to see with half an eye!" (John 9[:39–41], Isa. 6[:10]).[14]

The remedy for this miserable state of affairs in the world was simple and radical, according to Müntzer: Tyrants must be deposed; the common folk must become filled with the Holy Spirit; and a new John the Baptist must arise to prepare the way for Christ's final coming.

> If Christendom is to be restored at all, the usurious evildoers must be purged and, like dogs, must be made servants.... The poor common people must nurture the memory of the Spirit and thus learn to groan (Rom. 8[:22]) and pray and wait for a new John, a preacher full of grace who experienced faith by way of lack of faith. For they must know how an arch-unbeliever feels and how the measure of faith corresponds to the measure of diligent desire [for faith] (Eph. 4[:7–8], Psalm 67 [68:19]). If they did not, their inexperienced faith would be worse than the devil's slander against God in the abyss of hell.[15]

But, he added, a new John the Baptist must be even stronger than the original John the Baptist, because people were more obdurate (verstockt) than they had been. They were now to overcome the dead faith of Scripture and have their souls emptied of evil through suffering.

> In short, there is no other way: man must smash his stolen, simulated Christian faith by experiencing intense heartache, painful sadness, and indescribable wonder (Verwunderung). He will then feel very small and despise himself. The ungodly boast and are proud of such a state, but the elect drown in it. Only then can man elevate God and make Him great, and, after heartfelt sadness, enjoy Him as his savior. Then the great must make room for the small and be reduced to nothing before Him. Oh, if the poor rejected peasants knew this, they could surely profit from it!
>
> God despised bigwigs (grosse Hansen) like Herod, Caiaphas, and Ananias, and took into His service lowly people like Mary, Zachariah, and Elizabeth. Such is the work of God; and today He does the same thing.[16]

14. MSB 296:16–19.
15. MSB 296:21—297:7.
16. MSB 298:28—299:15.

Müntzer insisted that the church, like the individual, had to undergo inner turmoil and suffering before it could be renewed, but that this renewal was linked to a bitter struggle against faithless tyrants in both church and state. Only a preacher with true faith would be able to lead people out of bondage into freedom with God.

> Not everyone can have this office, even though he may have read every book; he must first know the certainty of his faith, as did those who wrote Scripture. Otherwise it is but the empty talk of thieves and a battle of words.[17]

People who were truly saved, who were overshadowed by the Holy Spirit, demonstrated their faith by living in a style separating them from the ungodly.

> The time of harvest is at hand (Matt. 9[:37]). Dear Brethren, the weeds are crying everywhere that it is not yet time for the harvest. The true Christianity of today will discover the right way, when temptations have passed (Matt. 18[:7–9]), for improvement follows temptation after the damage has been assessed and the pain of unbelief has passed. Today the Gospel will come into its own more than at the time of the apostles (Matt. 18[:11–12]). Many elect, from many lands and foreign nations, will be far superior to us lazy and negligent Christians.[18]

Church leaders, asserted Müntzer, were quick to accuse opposing voices of heretical "enthusiasm" *(Schwärmerei)*—Luther's favorite charge—but these charges were as old as Christianity itself. Indeed, Jesus himself was accused of falsely claiming to be the Messiah.

> Oh, how often the eternal Word has been hidden in the chosen people, in our Nazareth within Christendom, that is, in the flowering chosen ones who grow and bloom with the wisdom of the cross; and every lecherous pussyfooter has regarded them as foolish and mad.[19]

His convoluted argumentation and emotional rhetoric finally wound down with a summation.

17. MSB 307:20–27.
18. MSB 310:33—311:16.
19. MSB 316:36—317:6.

The sum of this first chapter [of Luke] is the strengthening of the Spirit in faith. It is nothing but this: the Most High God, our dear Lord, wants to give us the most high Christian faith by means of Christ's incarnation, so that we might become like Him in His suffering and life when we are overshadowed by the Holy Spirit, against whom the world sins and whom the world slanders in the crudest way. That is why [the Spirit] will be given only to the poor in spirit (who recognize their unbelief).

This conclusion is confirmed by the text of the entire chapter, and particularly by the blissful songs of praise sung by Mary and Zachariah [Luke 1:46–55, 67–79]. They speak quite clearly of the Spirit's kindliness, received through fear of God. The sacred covenant between God and Abraham, and all of us (Rom. 4[:3]) is to keep it, and to serve Him in holiness and justice, which will be true before Him. . . . May the Spirit of Christ help us. [Signed] A mockingbird mocking the ungodly.[20]

This treatise frightened the Weimar court, and the Nuremberg authorities confiscated as many copies as they could find. After all, Luther opposed Müntzer, and anyone who called for the forceful purging of the existing ecclesiastical and political governments could not expect much toleration. Müntzer, however, managed to disseminate the remaining copies of his treatise through the good offices of the travelling book dealer Hans Hut.[21]

When Müntzer arrived in the imperial city of Mühlhausen, perhaps on August 10, 1524,[22] he was welcomed by Henry Pfeiffer, the "Protestant" pastor of St. Mary's. Pfeiffer was an apostate monk who was engaged in a reform program similar to the one Müntzer had attempted in Zwickau. A native of

20. MSB 318:22—319:14, 24–25.

21. Hut was a member of the "League of the Elect" and later joined the peasants in their final battle against the princes in Frankenhausen. Müntzer had visited him on his way to Mühlhausen. See Gottfried Seebass, "Hans Hut, the Suffering Avenger" in Hans-Jürgen Goertz, ed., and Walter Klassen, English ed., *Radical Reformers, Biographical Sketches from Thomas Müntzer to Paracelsus* (Scottdale, Pa.: Herald Press, 1982), 55. E, 559 cites evidence for Müntzer's visit with Hut.

22. The journey from Allstedt to Mühlhausen usually took two to three days. My information about the city and Müntzer's activities there is derived from the chronicles researched by Reinhard Jordan, *Zur Geschichte der Stadt Mühlhausen in Thüringen 1523–1525*, Beiträge zum Jahresbericht des Gymnasiums in Mühlhausen, 2d ed. (Mühlhausen: Dannersche Buchdruckerei, 1908), and Otto Merx, *Thomas Müntzer und Heinrich Pfeiffer, 1523–1525* (Göttingen, W. Ger.: Vandenhoeck & Ruprecht, 1889).

Mühlhausen, he had gained immediate support from relatives and friends in a series of open meetings in the spring of 1523 at which he had begun his anti–Roman Catholic campaign. His activities had generated some violence and unrest, so the town council had banished him for a while. But by the beginning of August 1524 the town council, under pressure of influential citizens to adopt a new constitution granting unlimited freedom to any preacher in town, had permitted Pfeiffer to return.

The seventy-five hundred merchants, farmers, and clergy of Mühlhausen were sharply divided on the issues of ecclesiastical and social reforms, particularly on the participation of peasants in government.

Pfeiffer invited Müntzer to preach at St. Mary's, one of the two largest parishes in town. But Luther, in a letter dated August 21, 1524, had warned the town council against Müntzer, calling him a "false prophet" and prophesying that the result of his preaching would be "murder, rebellion, and bloodshed," just as in Allstedt.[23] Furthermore, Duke John had threatened Müntzer with another hearing if his preaching had the same effect it had had in Allstedt. As a result, the Mühlhausen town council did not welcome Müntzer's arrival.

Müntzer did not heed any of these warnings. He called for a radical transformation of the city into a community ruled by "the elect of God" from the pulpit, in private homes, and on the streets. He and Pfeiffer were assisted in this endeavor by one of the town's mayors. The mayor had had a man arrested on September 19 for slander during a wedding, but when the town council demanded a public hearing on the matter, the mayor and one of his colleagues left town.

Müntzer and Pfeiffer used the occasion to organize a demonstration to demand spiritual renewal in the face of the scandal in the mayor's office. More than two hundred citizens marched through the city carrying red crosses and swords, and camped outside Mühlhausen for a day, where they gained more support. On their return they demanded the transformation of Mühlhausen into a theocracy based on "eleven articles" they had drawn up with the aid of Müntzer and Pfeiffer. These articles

23. WA 15:329.3–5.

demanded the establishment of a new and "eternal" council, whose work was to be founded on the Word of God; a new city constitution; capital punishment to safeguard divine justice; and the immediate implementation of the new order.[24] But the new order could not be implemented, since there was too much confusion and unrest in the city. Groups of people assembled in homes to debate what to do; several members of the town council resigned.

In an attempt to overcome the confusion, Müntzer wrote an open letter to "the church of Mühlhausen." Speaking as "a servant of God,"[25] he told parishioners that their indecisiveness derived from fear.

> Since all this will come before the world in print, you will be blamed before all Christendom. It will be said that pious people did not obey the divine commandment, and that they have always had too much patience. And all of Christendom will not say about you what needs to be said about a chosen people in Deut. 4[:6–8], that "Surely this great nation is a wise and understanding people. It is a people that will rely on God, do right, and not fear the devil of this world with all his attacks, tricks, and boasting."[26]

He assured them that the new order would prevail, "for the common people (God be praised) almost everywhere have accepted the truth."[27]

The letter may have inflamed some groups. A village outside the city was put to the torch on September 26, 1524; the "leagues of the elect" were rumored to be ready to attack the city. However, the old town council somehow regained their position, elected two new mayors, and commanded supporters of law and order to mount a defense of the city from the city walls. When many people obeyed, the radicals dispersed, refusing to come to blows with the opposition. On September 27,

24. The articles are contained in Förstemann, *Neues Urkundenbuch*, 254–55. See also E, 581–83, where much of the work is attributed to the guild of weavers, though there is no solid evidence for such an assumption. Nor is there evidence to show that Müntzer organized a "league of the elect" or "eternal covenant" at this time, as suggested by Bräuer, "Thomas Müntzers Weg in den Bauernkrieg" in Demke, ed., *Thomas Müntzer.*

25. September 22, 1524. MSB 447—48.

26. MSB 448:12–19.

27. MSB 448:23–24.

1524, the city council banned Müntzer and Pfeiffer from the city. Müntzer had been in Mühlhausen just seven weeks.

Müntzer, accompanied by Pfeiffer, now headed for Nuremberg, where he hoped to finish a manuscript he had been working on, and to publish it with the help of Hans Hut. He intended this to be his final response to Luther's attacks, and when it was finally published, sometime before December 1524, it was entitled *A Highly Necessary Defense and Answer Against the Soft-Living Flesh of Wittenberg, Who in a Perverted Fashion Has So Miserably Soiled Pitiable Christendom with the Theft of Holy Scripture.*[28]

He stated he was writing from "the cave of Elijah, whose gravity *(Ernst)* spares no one (1 Kings 18 [19:9], Matt. 17[:1–8], Luke 1[:11, 26–38], Rev. 11[:3])." He applied Ps. 119:134 to himself: "Redeem me from human oppression that I may keep your precepts"; and, in imitation of Luther's *Letter to the Princes of Saxony Concerning the Rebellious Spirit,*[29] he dedicated his treatise to Christ, "To the most illustrious, firstborn Prince and almighty Lord, Jesus Christ, the gracious King of all kings, the brave Duke of all the faithful, my most gracious Lord and trusty protector, and to His sad and only bride, poor Christendom." He followed this dedication with laudatory references to Christ as the one who, in his Holy Spirit, empowers the elect and battles the devil within the scribes who allege to be his witnesses. "The greediest of all scribes" was Luther, the "Doctor Liar" who in his envy had abused Holy Scripture by attacking Müntzer, whom Christ had adopted and was using for his glorious purpose. As a disciple, however, he, Müntzer, would have to endure what the Lord himself had had to endure in the world, namely slanderous attacks.[30]

Throughout the treatise Müntzer tried to demonstrate that he rather than Luther interpreted Scripture correctly, since his own interpretation was based on the experiencing of the Holy

28. Text in MSB 322:343. English translation in Hans J. Hillerbrand, "Thomas Müntzer's Last Tract Against Luther," *The Mennonite Quarterly Review* 38 (1964) : 20–36.

29. WA 15:210. 3–6. LW 40:49.

30. MSB 323:4–21.

Spirit while Luther's interpretation was perverted by bookish reasoning.

> The whole Holy Scripture (as all creatures demonstrate as well) speaks of nothing but the crucified Son of God, who accordingly began to exercise His office at the time of Moses and who had to suffer and enter into the glory of His Father. This is clearly described in the final chapter of Luke [24:27, 44].... But the hateful scribes recognize none of this because they do not search Scripture with their heart and in the Spirit as they ought to do (Psalm 118 [119]), and as Christ commanded them to do (John 5[:39]). In this they are as learned as apes wishing to imitate the way the master makes shoes but only spoiling the leather. Why? Because they want to hear the Holy Spirit's consolation; yet they never in their lives reached bottom in their heart's sorrow, as they ought to do if the true light is to shine in darkness and give us the power to become children of God—clearly described in Psalms 54 [55:2–9] and 62 [63] and John 1[:4–5].[31]

Therefore, according to Müntzer, the scribes were like the ancient Pharisees who cried "Believe, believe" without having experienced the Holy Spirit in their hearts. They preached only for money. They declared that the law of Moses was abrogated and did not realize that the law, by causing the creature to suffer, led to true faith. But Luther did not want to hear the word "spirit," and called those who had the Spirit "swarming spirits" *(Schwimmelgeister).*[32]

> Like Moses, Christ began at the beginning and explained the law from beginning to end. That is why He says [John 8:12], "I am the light of the world." His preaching was so true and so well formulated that he captivated even the ungodly, through their human reason, as the evangelist Matthew writes in chapter 13[:54], and Luke also intimates in chapter 2[:47]. But since His teaching was too high for them, and Christ's person and life were too insignificant for them, they were offended by his teaching and by Him and muttered under their breath that he was a Samaritan and possessed by the devil. Their judgment was oriented to the flesh, which is just what the devil likes; and it had to be expressed so as to please the world which likes Brother Soft-Life (Job 28[:13?]). They

31. MSB 324:12–16, 23—325:2.
32. MSB 325:3—326:2.

arranged whatever they did in a way to please the world (Matt. 6[:1–5]) and 23[:5–7]).[33]

Müntzer proceeded to deride Luther, "the ungodly Wittenberg Flesh," for rejecting any positive value in the Old Testament law and teaching "justification by faith alone without the works of law," thus perverting the teaching of St. Paul.

> For only after one knows the law does the Spirit punish unbelief. No one recognizes unbelief unless he has embraced it as strongly as the most unbelieving heathen. Thus, by means of the law, all the elect have known their unbelief from the very beginning (Rom. 2[:12] and 7[:6–7]). I, together with all His members, take Christ to be the fulfillment of the law (Psalm 18 [19]). For it is through the observance of the law that God's will and His work must be done to the very end (Ps. 1[1–2], Rom. 2[:2]). Otherwise, just as the Jews with their Sabbath and their Scripture could in their simulated way never become aware of the depth, so no one would be able to separate faith from unbelief.[34]

Müntzer compared himself to the innocent dove that, unlike Luther the tricky raven, flies for the glory of God. Müntzer claimed to preach without any hidden agenda, and accused Luther of maliciously invoking the aid of the princes to hunt him down. Luther was the "Father Pussyfooter" when it came to telling the truth about Müntzer, who had clearly told the princes that God wanted them to use their swords to defend the godly against the ungodly. Luther flattered the world and its princes but misjudged Müntzer and misread St. Paul's gospel. Müntzer cautioned against Luther and those who might share Luther's attitude.

> In all of Christendom, all those who have become evildoers through the Fall must be justified by the law, as Paul says in Rom. 2[:12], so that the Father's wrath may purge the ungodly Christians who resist Christ's salvific teaching and time and space may be made for the just to learn God's will. If everyone could freely decide to use the law to punish sin, it would never be possible for a single Christian to engage in meditation [on God's will], for ungodly tyrants would be oppressing the innocent. The tyrants would use Scripture and say, "I have to martyr you. Christ suffered, and so you

33. MSB 326:13–24.
34. MSB 327:7–17.

must not resist" (Matt. 5[:39]). That would be a great perversion. Since the persecutors claim to be the best Christians, one must make careful distinctions.[35]

Only those who through the law experienced in their hearts the pain of purification from the sin of self-righteousness, and who subsequently experienced the power of the Holy Spirit to bring relief were the "elect" who could do God's will, that is, purge the ungodly with the sword.

Müntzer then accused Luther of perverting the proper distinction between law and gospel by attributing to the princes the work of the law. The princes used their power to oppress the godly instead of protecting them by punishing the ungodly. Thus Luther was "a Satan."[36] Nevertheless Luther could not obstruct the truth proclaimed by Müntzer, for people were beginning to join him rather than Luther. The orders of the "Wittenberg Pope" were no longer being obeyed.

> This Doctor Liar is naive when he writes that I should be prevented from preaching, or that you [princes] should see to it that the spirit of Allstedt refrain from hitting out. Look, dear brothers of Christ, see if he is learned. He is indeed! The world will in two or three years realize what murderous and malicious harm he has done. He writes that he will wash his hands of any guilt, so that no one might notice that he is a persecutor of truth. For he insists that his preaching is the true word of God because it causes persecution; I am truly amazed that this shameless monk can claim to be persecuted, when he drinks malmsey and eats the food of whores.[37]

Müntzer declared that he had expected a fair hearing and a debate, not this kind of malicious slander. Luther, he added, claimed to do everything according to the Word of God but ended up "a new Christ" defending clerical marriage. "I have been under your protection like a sheep is under the wolf's" (Matt. 10[:16]).[38] It was Luther, not he, who was the restless rebellious spirit who incited one prince to fight another.

35. MSB 330:14–25. The text is not as clear as it could be. Müntzer meant that only those who have experienced the punishment of the law in their hearts should be in charge of applying divine law to the world. Consequently the sword should be wielded by the godly and not the ungodly, since the latter use it for their own purposes rather than God's.

36. MSB 331:1–27.

37. MSB 333:21—334:6.

38. MSB 337:13–14.

He was particularly upset by Luther's criticism of visions and inner voices.

> He derides the divine word and makes much fun of me, saying that I hear heavenly voices and that angels speak to me, . . . I answer: I can only praise what the Almighty God does with me and what He says to me. I preach to the common people what is in Holy Scripture according to God's testimony, and I have no intention of preaching my own ideas. If I were to do so, I would welcome being called into account and punished by God and His dear friends. But I owe the scoffer nothing (Prov. 9[:7]).[39]

Debating with Luther as though he were present, Müntzer scoffed at Luther's experiences with church and state, claiming that Luther had fooled people at the Leipzig debate in 1519, by fleeing the city after having enjoyed good wine; had lied when he claimed to have silenced Müntzer and the Zwickau prophets Storch and Stübner; and had not been a hero at Worms in 1521, since German nobles had protected him after he had flattered them.[40]

> If one did not see through your villainy, one would swear by all the saints that you are a pious Martin. Sleep softly, dear flesh! I'd rather smell you through God's wrath roasting in your obstinacy in the oven or in the pot on the fire (Jer. 1[:13]) than have you cooked in your own juices. May the devil devour you (Ezek. 23[:46–47]). You are ass meat, and it would take too long to cook you until you are tender; you remain a tough dish for your sucklings.[41]

He closed with a reference to the Weimar hearing which, he asserted, had maliciously interfered with his preaching, adding that he, like David, would overcome the Goliath.[42] In an appendix, he predicted—in both Latin and German—that the common people would be liberated from the satanic wiles of "Doctor Liar."

> Oh Doctor Liar, you sly fox, you have with your lies saddened the hearts of the righteous, whom God did not make sad. You have

39. MSB 338:17–24.
40. MSB 340:22—341:4.
41. MSB 341:27—342:2.
42. MSB 342:17—343:4.

therefore strengthened the power of the ungodly, so that they have maintained their old ways. That is why what happens to a fox in a trap will happen to you: the people will become free, and God will be their only Lord.[43]

Müntzer's demonization of Luther was a response to Luther's demonization of Müntzer. Polemics took its toll, and the two reformers finished in a swamp of mutual slander. In a letter to his good friend Christoph Meinhard in Eisleben, Müntzer reflected one more time on his relationship with Luther: "I have become a stench to the world, to the disgrace of the soft-living brothers of pussyfooters."[44] This was an admission that Luther had made his life quite difficult. Still, he held on to the conviction that he, too, had created problems for the Wittenbergers. He claimed that he could have caused all kinds of problems in Nuremberg if he had really wanted to incite the people, but that he had preferred the printed word.[45] It is quite likely that Müntzer took so little public action because Henry Pfeiffer's attempts to organize people met with such heavy resistance.

On October 29, 1524, the Nuremberg city council recommended that Pfeiffer be expelled if he continued to propagate Müntzer's "enthusiasm" (Schwärmerei).[46] The city of Nuremberg respected Luther, and Luther's opposition to Müntzer was well known. As a result, Müntzer left Nuremberg sometime in November of 1524, and turned his face southwest toward Switzerland.

43. MSB 343:5–14.

44. Letter written sometime in November or December 1524. MSB 449:11–13.

45. MSB 450:12–17.

46. From the minutes of the city council, cited in Theodor Kolde, "Hans Denck und die gottlosen Maler von Nürnberg," Beiträge zur bayrischen Kirchengeschichte 8 (1901): 12, n. 1. There is no clear evidence to show that Müntzer was in close contact with the small Anabaptist community in Nuremberg or with Hans Denck in particular. See the analysis of the evidence in E, 628–29.

7

RADICAL AMONG REBELS

It is difficult to reconstruct Müntzer's journey to southwestern Germany and northern Switzerland between October 1524 and February 1525. He did have good reason to turn to Switzerland for support, for northern Switzerland, under the leadership of the reformers Ulrich Zwingli (1484–1531) in Zurich and John Oecolampadius (1482–1531) in Basel, had become Protestant. There were also some "Brethren of Zurich," nicknamed "Anabaptists" because they rebaptized, who had made contact with Müntzer by letter on September 5, 1524.[1]

Conrad Grebel, the Anabaptist leader, had written to Müntzer because he and others in the movement had read some of his writings and had resonated to his assertion that Christendom confused divine with human power. But the Brethren criticized Müntzer's "Catholic" liturgical tendencies and rejected his advocacy of the sword to advance the gospel. "True faithful Christians are sheep among wolves," Müntzer was told, "[they are] sacrificial lambs who must be baptized by fear, misery, persecution, suffering and dying."[2] However, Grebel told Müntzer he was right in condemning infant baptism as being against Scripture and hoped that he would join them in advocating an adult baptism based on faith. He added that the Zurich Brethren,

1. MSB 437—45. English translation in Walter Rauschenbusch, "The Zurich Anabaptists and Thomas Müntzer," *The American Journal of Theology* 11 (1905): 91–106; and in Williams and Mergal, eds., *Spiritual and Anabaptist Writers*, 71–85.
2. MSB 442:29–31.

Carlstadt, and Müntzer could make common cause to correct Luther's misguided reform movement.[3]

In his 1525 prison confession, Müntzer stated that he had been with rebellious peasants near Basel, in Klettgau and Hegau, and that he had become acquainted with Oecolampadius.[4] In a report to his friend Willibald Pirkheimer in Nuremberg, Oecolampadius wrote that Müntzer had appeared with a friend named Hugowaldius, that they had stayed for a meal, and that they had conversed about the cruciform life and the relationship between temporal government and the rule of Christ. He denied having had any interest in the kind of conspiracy Müntzer had advocated. But since the letter was written after Müntzer's execution in May of 1525, and Müntzer was known as a condemned rebel, a certain amount of caution on his part is quite understandable.

Müntzer decided to return to Mühlhausen sometime in February 1525, convinced that this would be the strongest base for a realization of his ideals. On his way back, he was arrested in Fulda, just west of the Thuringian forest. He was not held long, but since Fulda was just recovering from the unrest caused by the preaching of a priest sympathetic to Luther's cause, any public utterance Müntzer made would be considered a threat to peace.[5]

Pfeiffer had returned to Mühlhausen in December 1524, and his attempts to drive Catholics from the city had met with strong support from both peasants and burghers.[6] By February Pfeiffer had succeeded in making the city "evangelical," and was influential in having Müntzer called to St. Mary's Church as pastor. Müntzer now had an audience ready to listen to him. There were rumors that he and Pfeiffer intended to become members of the city council in order to dictate the city's policy, but the attempt was unsuccessful if it was made. But they were successful in persuading the council to call up all able-bodied

3. MSB 444:23–28, 445:4–7.

4. Confession, 1525. MSB 544:11–18. The best reconstruction of Müntzer's journey is found in E, 630–75, and includes speculations about possible contacts with rebellious peasants.

5. The Allstedt official Hans Zeiss reported the arrest to George Spalatin on February 22, 1525. AGBM 2, 66.

6. Ibid.

men to defend the city against a rumored attack by the arch-Catholic Duke George of Saxony and Luther's friend Philip of Hesse. Müntzer used the occasion to address a meeting of a troop of recruits. He demanded that they swear to die for the Word of God if necessary, but the troop's captain discouraged the men from taking any such oath.[7]

Müntzer and Pfeiffer held meetings for large crowds of agitated citizens in St. Mary's Church, and succeeded in having a new city council elected by March 17, 1525. This "Eternal Council" now began to reorganize the city for further action against Catholics and feudal landlords. Men were recruited and trained for service in the military, and guns and other weapons were manufactured. They designed a banner of their own: a rainbow on a white ground, inscribed with the words *verbum domini maneat in eternum*, "the Word of God will remain forever." This banner was kept on exhibition behind the altar of St. Mary's Church, an obvious symbol of Müntzer's "eternal league" that would transform the world into a place ruled by the Word of God alone.

There was increasing unrest in southern Germany and the Austrian Alps, where the peasants were rebelling. This German peasants' rebellion of 1524–25, labeled a "rustic tumult" *(tumultus rusticorum)* by many observers, was the culmination of persistent regional tensions between princes and common people.[8] The process of urbanization and the rise of commerce based on the exchange of currency rather than barter had placed a burden on the peasants. The old Teutonic code of law had allowed serfs to own part of the land they tilled for their feudal landlords, and to keep a share of what the land produced. The introduction of money and the modification of local laws to

7. Evidence from the city chronicles, cited in E, 684–85.

8. For an assessment of the peasants' rebellion, based on massive research, see Heiko A. Oberman, "The Gospel of Social Unrest: 450 Years After the So-Called 'German Peasants' War' of 1525," *Harvard Theological Review* 69 (1976): 103–9. Oberman stresses the religious aspect of the rebellion, contending that if Luther had not made Müntzer the culprit of the rebellion others, like Hans Hut, would be better recognized as its religious leaders (ibid., 123). He proposes the designation "social unrest" or "rustic agitation" rather than "peasants' war" because the two sides were quite unequal. The princes used their war machine (state-of-the-art weapons) while the peasants had few modern weapons and fought with tools such as flails, sickles, and pitchforks.

conform to Roman law had added to the peasants' hardship. According to Roman law, the legal status of a person was defined in terms of ownership of private property, and peasants were barred from owning property. Moreover, peasants were asked to deliver more agricultural goods to market so that the feudal landlords could afford to compete in trade and pay their own taxes. Since there were many independent princes of small individual territories in Germany, the burden of feudalism was particularly heavy on peasants because of the fierce competition among them.

It is not surprising that Martin Luther's teaching awakened in the peasants a desire not only for the old Germanic tradition of individual freedom, but also for liberation from the yoke of a feudalism permeated by the intrusion of foreign ecclesiastical and secular powers in German affairs. Luther's view of the common priesthood of all believers, which was centered in the conviction that, based on baptism, every vocation constitutes a form of priesthood, appealed to both German nobles and peasants. The nobles found in it their justification for revolting against the empire (as some of them had done in 1523); the peasants regarded it as their vindication for fighting for their ancient right to own part of the soil they tilled. They now combined this demand for the "old law," the Teutonic code, with a call for the "divine law" expressed in the Bible, which Luther regarded as the canon for reform.[9]

The rising unrest in southern and southwestern Germany convinced Müntzer that this was a clear sign of radical change from the status quo to the promised rule of God. His elect, who had experienced internal purification, were now moving to purify the world from evil. He was not alone in this view. On the basis of the constellation of the stars and planets, others had the same expectations. On the basis of a particular Pisces constellation he had discovered, a Tübingen mathematician had predicted a deluge to occur in February 1524 which would threaten the whole

9. Günther Franz, *Der deutsche Bauernkrieg*, 6th ed. (Darmstadt: Wissenschaftliche Buchgesellschaft, 1962 [1st ed., 1933], 41–42) points out that the struggle for the "old law" was characterized by spontaneous mass rebellions in specific regions, whereas the struggle for "divine law" involved conspiracies and small rebellious movements like Müntzer's "league."

world. George Tannstätter, a Viennese astrologer, predicted peasant uprisings to take place in Austria after 1515, declaring that these would be the beginning of unrest between the clergy and the common people. A proverb of the time said, "Whoever does not die in 1523, drown in 1524, or is not beaten to death in 1525 can truly speak of miracles."[10] When the promised deluge failed to occur in 1524, popular imagination fastened on the peasants' uprisings in northern Switzerland, southern Germany, and the Austrian Alps. Woodcuts appeared which showed pope, emperor, and bishops being threatened by armed peasants in brilliant sunlight under a flag showing a peasant shoe (a *Bundschuh*, which is laced, rather than the boot worn by nobles).

The Swabian peasants made their demands known in the *Twelve Articles* they drew up between February 28 and March 1, 1525. Many groups of peasants subscribed to these *Articles* even though they could not agree on all points.[11] The demands, annotated with biblical quotations in the margins, were:

1. The right of a congregation to elect and depose a pastor, who should preach the gospel "without any human additions."

2. The collection of the "major tithe" by the church, to be used to pay the pastor, and the abolition of the "minor tithe," a tax on farm animals, "because God, the Lord, created animals to be freely used by human creatures."

3. The right to be free individuals, because Christ redeemed everyone, peasants as well as kings, and the Bible admonishes persons to obey political authority only insofar as it does not condone serfdom.

4. The right to hunt and fish within the boundaries of the fief

10. Quoted, along with other evidence, in Günther Franz, *Der deutsche Bauernkrieg*, 92.

11. Text in Alfred Götze, ed., "Die zwölf Artikel der Bauern 1525," *Historische Vierteljahrschrift* 5 (1902): 1–33. English translation in Luther's *Admonition to Peace, A Reply to the Twelve Articles of the Peasants in Swabia*, 1525. LW 46:8–16. The *Twelve Articles* was written by Sebastian Lotzer, the official scribe for the Baltringen peasants. Müntzer cannot be linked to the writing of them. See Günther Franz, "Die Entstehung der 'Zwölf Artikel' der deutschen Bauernschaft," ARG 36 (1939): 193–213, esp. 209. See also the extensive discussion of their origins and content in E, 653–71.

"because God has made humans the lords over all animals ever since creation."

5. The right to draw wood for fuel from the forest.
6. A reduction in the amount of work done without compensation for the landlord, whose increasing demands violated ancient practice, and a return to the old custom of labor done "according to the prescription of the Word of God"—six days of labor and one day of rest.
7. Protection against the landlord's increasing demands.
8. Enactment of laws to determine the proper feudal obligations of each vassal "so that the peasant does not work for nothing."
9. Punishment of a crime in accordance with established justice rather than at the whim of the landlord.
10. Use of some meadows and fields as common property, in accordance with the old custom.
11. Assistance for widows and orphans unable to support themselves.
12. "The right to be judged in all demands in accordance with the Bible."

Luther first applauded the willingness of the peasants to be instructed by Holy Scripture and to have their demands judged by it. He also criticized the princes, as well as bishops and other landlords, for having hardened hearts in the matter of agricultural reforms. But Luther would not tolerate the term "Christian" for any rebellion or for violence of any kind. He pleaded with both princes and peasants to come to some understanding in good Christian conscience. But his advice fell on deaf ears, especially since the princes refused to negotiate with the peasants as a matter of principle. When the peasants finally revolted, Luther attacked them and asserted that they had fallen into the hands of Satan. He contended that order had to be preserved at all cost, and he applauded the princes for using the sword to put down the rebellion.[12]

---

12. Luther's positive attitude toward the peasants is documented in *Admonition to Peace, A Reply to the Twelve Articles of the Peasants in Swabia*, 1525. WA 18:292–334. LW 46:5–43. For his condemnation of the rebellion as "satanic," see *Against the Robbing and Murderous Peasants*, 1525. WA 18:384–401. LW 46:47–61.

What seemed diabolic to Luther was to Müntzer God-willed. When Müntzer heard of sporadic uprisings in the vicinity of Mühlhausen, he made an emotional appeal to his former parishioners in Allstedt to crusade against the tyranny of the political status quo.

How long are you going to sleep? How long will you refuse to yield to the will of God because you think He might have forsaken you? Oh, how often have I told you how it must be, that God would not reveal Himself unless you yield [gelassen]! If you don't, your sacrifice, your heartache, will be in vain. You then must again experience suffering. I tell you, if you refuse to suffer for God's sake, you will become the devil's martyrs.[13]

He admonished the Allstedters that the external transformation of the world was at hand.

Begin to fight the fight of the Lord! It is high time. Urge all the brethren not to deride the divine testimony. Otherwise they will all perish. All of Germany, France, and Switzerland has been awakened. The Master wants to start the game. It is the villains' turn: four monastic churches were devastated during Easter week; the peasants in the Klettgau and Hegau have risen up, three thousand strong, and the band is growing.[14]

Even if there are only three of you who trust God and seek only to honor Him, you need not fear a hundred thousand. At them! At them! [Dran, dran] The time is now. The villains are as desperate as dogs.... Have no consideration for the misery of the ungodly. They will beg and whine like children. Do not be merciful. Do as Moses did under the mandate of God (Deut. 7[:1–5]). He has commanded us to do the same. Call on the villages and towns, especially on the miners and their friends, who will do well. We must not sleep any longer.[15]

He mentioned some Allstedters who had joined his league, and again urged others to join him.

Get going, while the fire is hot! Do not let your sword cool, do not lay it down. Use your hammers on the anvil of Nimrod (Gen. 10:8) and destroy their tower.... At them! At them, while you still have the day. God marches ahead of you. Follow, follow! It is all recorded

13. MSB 454:1–8. The letter may have been written on April 26 or 27, 1525.
14. MSB 454:10–16.
15. MSB 454:19–21, 24—455:2.

in Matthew 24, Ezekiel 34, Daniel 7, Ezra 10, Revelation 6, which all explain Romans 13.[16]

He was convinced that this crusade of peasants and burghers against the oppressive forces of the status quo was the final struggle before the end of the world, as had been prophesied in Scripture. He signed this letter, "a servant of God against the ungodly."[17]

Hoping to unite with other groups of rebellious peasants, Müntzer and Pfeiffer on April 26, 1525, moved from Mühlhausen to Langensalza—a few miles southeast of the city—with about four hundred armed men. But many Mühlhausen citizens not only stayed behind, they alerted the people of Langensalza of impending childish political actions and warned them against "false preachers," presumably Müntzer and Pfeiffer.[18]

The militant Mühlhausen group found little support in Langensalza, so they plundered and devastated a monastery nearby. A peasant who had participated in this action later confessed that Müntzer had ordered the destruction as an example for what would be done to all nobles and their possessions.[19] The Mühlhausen chronicle reported that Müntzer praised a group of peasants who had robbed a monastery, and that he supervised the distribution of the spoils among the rebels in an encampment in Görmar.[20]

Müntzer heard of unrest in nearby Frankenhausen, and encouraged the Frankenhausen congregation to join his uprising: "Be of good courage, and trust in God alone. He will give more strength to your small group than you will be able to believe."[21] By May 4, even some nobles promised their support, among them Count Günther of Schwarzburg, whom Müntzer commended for his sense of justice.[22]

Electoral Commissioner Hans Zeiss on May 7 reported to

16. MSB 455: 14–16, 18–21.

17. MSB 456:7.

18. MSB 458:16–21. Letter from the Mühlhausen congregation to Langensalza dated April 30, 1525.

19. MSB 457:13–14.

20. Quoted in E, 707.

21. Letter dated April 29, 1525. MSB 458:3–5.

22. Letter dated May 4, 1525. MSB 459:9–10.

RADICAL AMONG REBELS   101

Elector Frederick that large bands of rebels throughout the region had plundered thirty monasteries, that about fifteen thousand rebels had gathered in or near Mühlhausen, and that some nobles had joined them.[23] He was not aware that Frederick had died on May 5, 1525. The prince had told John, his brother and successor, that the rebellion might be a sign of God's wrath because of the heavy burdens laid on the poor peasants.[24]

Despite the distortion of facts and figures created by legend and rumor, the final phase of what has been called the German Peasants' War can be reconstructed with some fidelity from various sources.[25] Müntzer himself lacked precise information regarding the extent of the rebellion when he and Pfeiffer led their followers from Mühlhausen to join with other bands. However, his assumption that a large-scale rebellion was indeed in progress was basically correct. About sixty thousand peasants and burghers had risen up against their feudal landlords in Thuringia, and there were uprisings in many territories ranging from the Harz Mountains to Switzerland and Austria. The rulers of these territories were slow to react to these events. Some, like Landgrave Philip of Hesse, George of Saxony, Henry of Brunswick, and Elector John finally managed to raise a well-equipped army of several thousand men.

On May 7, 1525, Müntzer returned to Mühlhausen to drum up more support for what he was convinced would be the Holy League of the Elect's last battle against the ungodly of this world. He wrote to the Mühlhausen city council and to the congregations in Smalcald, Sonderhausen, and Eisenach, all of them neighboring cities. His message was simple and clear: Victory would be on the side of the rebels despite some defections. "Be of the best courage and sing with us, 'I am not afraid of hundreds [ten] of thousands of people round about who have set themselves against me' [Ps. 3:7]."[26] He told the Eisenach

23. Günther Franz, ed., *Quellen zur Geschichte des Bauernkrieges*, Ausgewählte Quellen zur deutschen Geschichte der Neuzeit, Freiherr von Stein-Gedäctnisausgabe 2 (Munich: Oldenburg, 1963), 515–16 (no. 177).

24. Letter dated April 14, 1525. AGBM 2:91 (no. 1183).

25. The most detailed but also most confusing analysis is offered in E, chap. 9. A good overview is provided by Bräuer, "Thomas Müntzers Weg in den Bauernkrieg," 76–80, and by Franz, *Der deutsche Bauernkrieg*, esp. 248–70.

26. May 7, 1525, letter to the Christian Brethren of Smalcald. MSB 461:18–21.

congregation that the prophesy of Dan. 7[:27] "that power will be given to the common people" had now been fulfilled. He signed the letter "Thomas Müntzer, with the sword of Gideon."[27]

On May 11, Müntzer again left town, leading his troop to Frankenhausen, located halfway between Mühlhausen and Allstedt, for this is where he, like Gideon [Judg. 7:6], intended to help fight the ungodly of this world. The troop carried the Holy League's banner, the rainbow symbol of the divine covenant. Some chroniclers reported two other banners carried by the Mühlhausen group, one a drawn sword to depict the annihilation of the ungodly, and the other a red cross to demonstrate the suffering of God's elect.

He continued writing letters from the rebel camp near Frankenhausen. His chief targets of derision were Ernest and Albrecht, the counts of Mansfeld. The chaplain to the rebels wrote to Count Ernest:

> I, Thomas Müntzer, formerly pastor in Allstedt, admonish you, for the sake of the name of the living God, to end your tyrannical raging. You have begun to torture Christians. You have scolded the holy Christian faith, calling it a knavery. You have aimed to destroy the Christians. So speak up, you miserable and poor bag of maggots, who made you a prince of the people whom God has obtained with his dear blood? You have to prove you are a Christian. You must prove your faith, as 1 Pet. 3[:8–12] commands.[28]

He then announced that Count Ernest would be treated like a Turk unless he recanted his evil ways:

> So that you may know that we are under strict orders, I will tell you: the eternal, living God has mandated that you shall be thrown off your seat by force and be turned over to us. For you are of no use to Christendom; you are a dust mop harmful to the friends of God. God has spoken of you and the likes of you in Ezekiel 34 and 39, Daniel 7, Matthew 3. The prophet Obadiah [4] says that your nest must be torn apart and destroyed.[29]

Müntzer wrote to Count Albrecht of Mansfeld in the same manner. He prophesied that Albrecht's demise would be the fulfillment of Mary's "magnificat" (Luke 1:52):

27. May 9 letter. MSB 464:17.
28. May 12, 1525. MSB 467:16—468:5.
29. MSB 468:25–31.

He has put down the mighty from their thrones and exalted those of low degree (whom you despise). Couldn't you find what Ezekiel prophesied in chapter 37 in your Lutheran gruel or Wittenberg soup? You are equally unable to taste, in your Martinian peasant dung, what the same prophet prophesied in chapter 39[:7–20]: God commands all the birds of heaven to devour the flesh of princes, and unintelligent animals to drink the blood of the bigwigs. This is written in the secret revelations of verses 18–19. Do you think God cares more about you tyrants than about His people?[30]

He concluded with the threat that unless Albrecht ceded political power to the people, he, like Ernest, would be treated like an archenemy of the Christian faith.[31]

The only available evidence to support accusations of murder made against the rebels was the execution on May 13, following a brief trial in the encampment, of four of Count Ernest's subjects.[32] On Sunday, May 14, 1525, a small group of rebels encountered an advance troop of men under Philip of Hesse and Henry of Brunswick outside of Frankenhausen, but there was little military action.

Müntzer preached his last sermon on that same day, the last of a series of three which, according to Hut's later recollection, had focused on the notion that the rebellion was the final event leading to the world's purification from sin and oppression.

God the Almighty wants to purify the world now. He has taken power from the government and has given it to the subjects. The princes in their weakness will beg for mercy, but they should not be believed because they cannot be trusted. God is with them [the subjects]. The peasants painted a rainbow on all their flags, and Müntzer told them it symbolizes the covenant with God. After he had preached for three days, a rainbow appeared around the sun, and Müntzer told the peasants that this was a sign that God was on their side, and that they should be brave and fight confidently.[33]

30. May 12, 1525, letter. MSB 469:15—470:5.

31. MSB 470:7–13.

32. The chronicles suggest that Müntzer had a leading role in the event and that he certainly approved the execution. See AGBM 2:888. On the basis of various sources, E, 762–67 asserts that Müntzer may have invoked the "divine law" of the Bible (ibid., 764). In his "confession under torture," Müntzer admitted that he had agreed with the rebels' judgment, but had been motivated "by fear." See MSB 547:11–13.

33. Text of the confession of Hans Hut, 1527. AGBM 2:897.

Several places near Frankenhausen indeed observed what astronomers call a "halo" on May 15, 1525. Sixteenth-century chronicles called them "rainbows."[34]

On Monday, May 15, the rebels took up a defensive position on a hill known as the "house mountain" *(Hausberg)* outside of Frankenhausen. Their main line of defense was a barricade composed of wagons. They sent a message to the princes to convey their just cause:

> We confess Jesus Christ. We are not here to hurt anyone (John 2) but to preserve divine justice. Nor are we here to shed blood. We will not hurt you if you do not do so either. Everyone should agree to this.[35]

Whether this message was an offer to negotiate a peace settlement or a response to an offer from the princes, who were trying to gain time in order to mount a devastating assault, cannot be determined with certainty.[36] But the princes' official response left no doubt about their intention:

> If you hand over the false prophet Thomas Müntzer alive, as well as his followers, and if you surrender unconditionally, we shall treat you accordingly and show you the mercy appropriate to the circumstances [*nach Gelegenheit der Sachen*]. We desire a speedy answer.[37]

The peasants refused. It was said that Müntzer rode from one small group to another to encourage those who doubted the outcome of the impending battle. Some young miners recalled that he had shouted to them to trust in the power of God.[38]

The princes, having combined their troops, surrounded the rebel position and attacked with heavy artillery. The cavalry and

34. "Halos" are phenomena of "atmospheric optics." See Diedrich Wattenberg, "Der Regenbogen von Frankenhausen am 15. Mai 1525 im Lichte anderer Himmelserscheinungen," *Vorträge und Schriften der Archenhold-Sternwarte Berlin-Treptow* 24 (Berlin, 1965), esp. 3.

35. MSB 472:7–11.

36. It has been suggested that Philip of Hesse offered to negotiate and that some rebel leaders agreed to do so. See Manfred Bensing, *Thomas Müntzer und der Thüringer Aufstand 1525* (Berlin: Deutscher Verlag der Wissenschaften, 1966), 221. E, 771–74 refutes this suggestion, instead arguing that the text originated with Müntzer, who offered the princes a last chance to join his cause.

37. MSB 473:1–5.

38. AGBM 2:378.

then the infantry attacked next. There was panic when the first bullets hit the wagon barricade. Many of the peasants and miners tried to escape into the town, but were intercepted. About five thousand rebels were killed, six hundred were captured, and a few hundred, among them Hans Hut, escaped. The princes lost six men. The battle resulted in a massacre.

Müntzer managed to flee into Frankenhausen, but he was captured shortly thereafter. Luther received a report of the capture from his friend John Rühel, written on May 26.

> Müntzer was hiding in a house close to the town gate. He had taken off his coat and climbed into a bed. The Saxon nobleman Otto of Eppe entered the house by chance to set up his quarters there; and by chance his servant went to the attic, saw someone in bed, and called the squire. He asked, "Who is there? Who are you?" He answered, "Oh, I am a poor sick man." Then (by looking around as people do) he found his [Müntzer's] bag and in it the letter Count Albrecht had sent to the camp. He said, "How come you have this letter? You must be the priest." He first denied it, then confessed and was taken along to Duke George [of Saxony]. They sat him on a bench, with the duke next to him asking why he had had four men beheaded on the previous Saturday. He answered that divine law, not he, had done it.[39]

After a while Duke Henry of Brunswick joined in the interrogation, debating the biblical basis for Müntzer's views and quoting the New Testament while Müntzer quoted the Old Testament.[40]

Müntzer was taken to Heldrungen Castle the same day, May 15. This was the headquarters of Count Ernest of Mansfeld, and Müntzer was questioned the next day. The minutes of this interrogation were published as a "Confession" *(Bekenntnis)*.[41] The first part listed fifteen confessions:

1. Müntzer had little regard for the power of the Eucharist as an external means of salvation.
2. He had presided over eucharistic celebrations and had offered the sacrament to the sick [a "Catholic" custom, thus revealing Müntzer's inconsistency].

39. Text ibid., 378–79. Also in E, 787.
40. Ibid.
41. Text in MSB 544—49.

3. He had been in Switzerland, but had not participated in uprisings.
4. Owners of castles oppressed their subjects.
5. The nobility should be limited in the number of horses they could possess—dukes should have eight, counts four, and minor nobles no more than two to ride.
6. A number of people [some are listed] belonged to Müntzer's "league," which opposed the enemies of the gospel.
7. He had been asked by the preacher of Sangershausen to draft a letter to the congregation urging them to persecute the enemies of the gospel.
8. In Weimar he had met Dr. Strauss, who contended that the Lutherans confused people, and had made contact with people in Mühlhausen.
9. He had attacked Count Ernest of Mansfeld because the count refused to have the Word of God preached to his subjects.
10. He had found supporters in Mühlhausen.
11. He had been at Mallerbach when the chapel there had been destroyed [during his Allstedt days], and had branded the place an abomination.
12. He knew of the destruction of a house in Mühlhausen, a destruction provoked by the peasants' "Twelve Articles."
13. The city council of Mühlhausen had refused to join the league.
14. Nicholas Storch and Max Stübner had been with Luther in Wittenberg, but Müntzer had not been with them when Luther criticized them.
15. A preacher had joined the rebellion and had led rebel groups.[42]

There was not much new that the princes could use to demonstrate how heretical and seditious Müntzer was. But under torture Müntzer divulged more information, which the minutes summarized in twelve segments:

42. MSB 544—547:5. This reference to Dr. James Strauss, pastor in Eisenach, does not disclose much about his role in the hearing that Müntzer had in Weimar. Strauss had some interest in economic matters and may have been called in by the Saxon court to evaluate Müntzer's economic views. The best guesses are found in Hinrichs, *Luther und Müntzer*, 84–89.

1. The names of Zwickau citizens in Müntzer's league.
2. Heinrich Pfeiffer's proposal to destroy all but one castle in each region.
3. Müntzer's condonation, "out of fear," of the execution at the rebel camp.
4. The names of co-conspirators from Mühlhausen.
5. Plans for Ernest of Mansfeld's execution if he was captured.
6. The purpose of the rebellion, which was to make everyone equal in Christendom and thus depose princes.
7. A list of Allstedt members in Müntzer's league.
8. The purpose of the league to share goods according to need and to kill princes opposed to this purpose.
9. A list of the Mansfeld members of the league and the name of the person who had the rest of the list in Allstedt.
10. The admission that in his youth in Aschersleben Müntzer had created a league against Archbishop Ernest.
11. His plan to create a territory of a ten-mile radius around Mühlhausen for his league.
12. The admission that Mühlhausen had provided eight artillery pieces for the rebels, and Stolberg had lent one.[43]

The greatest gain for the princes from this confession under torture was the names of other rebels.

The Wittenbergers were dissatisfied with the results of the interrogation. Luther complained that Müntzer had not been asked the right questions, and Philip Melanchthon wondered why Müntzer had not been asked about the revelations he had received—whether he had invented them or had received them from Satan.[44]

Anticipating his execution, Müntzer dictated a letter on May 17 to friends in Mühlhausen from his prison in Heldrungen. He asked them to take care of his wife and to dispose of his possessions, consisting mostly of books and clothes. He then alluded to the defeat of the peasants in Frankenhausen.

Dear Brethren, it is good that you did not receive the same blow

43. MSB 547:5—549:12.
44. Luther's letter to John Rühel, dated May 30, 1525. WA.BR 3:515.28. Melanchthon in *Die Historie Thomae Müntzers*, St.L 16:173.

they suffered at Frankenhausen. That defeat was undoubtedly caused by the fact that everyone strove more for selfishness than for the justification of Christianity.... I have often warned you that God's punishment cannot be avoided; it will be done by government unless one recognizes the harm done. Such harm can be avoided. Therefore be friendly with everyone and do not embitter government any longer, as many have done in their selfishness. May the grace of Christ and His Spirit be with you.... I will no longer give occasion to rebellion, now in my last days, so that my soul be no longer burdened and no more innocent blood be shed.[45]

He then made a final statement in the presence of six nobles which was later published as his "Recantation" *(Widerruf)*. The statement included a notation that this was what he honestly wanted to say, since it was made without pressure on him. The recantation declared:

First, that he had preached against the obedience due to government, with the result that his hearers and other subjects became involved with him in blasphemous rebellion and disobedience. He therefore asks that God's will be offended no longer and that government be obeyed, as is ordained by God. This should be granted to him.

Second, since he had preached in many and erroneous ways about the blessed sacrament of the holy corpus Christi, as well as against the common order of the church, he now desires to hold to the teachings of the church as they have always been, and to die as a reconciled member of the church, adhering to it in unity and peace. This he wants to confess before God and the whole world, asking God that he be forgiven as a brother.

Finally, he requests that his letter to Mühlhausen be sent off and that his wife and child receive all his belongings.[46]

It is difficult to assess this statement. Did Müntzer really recant, as his enemies claimed? Did torture force him to change his mind? Did he actually say what the princes' scribes wrote down as "confession" and "recantation"? Did he interpret the defeat at Frankenhausen as God's final test of the "elect" who had tried to remain faithful but been ultimately abandoned by God? There are no satisfactory answers to these questions.

But it does seem that Müntzer viewed this battle as a divinely

45. Dated May 17, 1525. MSB 473:18–21, 474:1–6, 18–21.
46. MSB 550.

willed event to test the enduring tension between sinful self-ishness and true faith. Moreover, he apparently viewed himself and his Mühlhausen friends as failures because they escaped martyrdom in battle. Müntzer may have succumbed to his enemies in the torture chamber of Heldrungen Castle. The evidence produced by these enemies suggests that he abandoned his vision, but this evidence may reflect more on the cruelty of the torturers than on Müntzer's loss of vision. Four years later, in the course of a conversation about the peasants' rebellion, Philip of Hesse stated that Müntzer had not recanted his views but that he had asked God's forgiveness for some errors. Philip, who was twenty years old when he met Müntzer in prison, seemed impressed by the way Müntzer faced his own death.[47]

The princes' army marched on Mühlhausen after pillaging Frankenhausen. The Mühlhausen city council surrendered the city to the dukes, who ordered the arrest of a number of rebel leaders, and imposed payment of reparation on the city. They then declared it a fief of George and Elector John, the dukes of Saxony, and of Philip of Hesse.

Henry Pfeiffer fled the city on May 21, along with about three hundred members of the "league of the elect," but he was captured near Eisenach shortly afterwards. On Saturday, May 27, Müntzer and Pfeiffer were beheaded in Camp Görmar. Their separated bodies and heads were exhibited on stakes outside the city of Mühlhausen, as a warning to those left alive.

---

47. From the notes of the Strassbourg preacher Caspar Hedio, who had heard Philip speak about Müntzer at a dinner on September 29, 1529. See A. Erichson, "Strassburger Beiträge zur Geschichte des Marburger Religionsgesprächs," ZKG 4 (1881): 418. E, 803, conjectures that Müntzer did not recant, being convinced that the issue was obedience to God's law rather than "social agitation." Bensing (*Thomas Müntzer*, 92) speaks of Müntzer's unbroken faith in the ability of the common people to liberate themselves from oppression—a conjecture influenced by a Marxist philosophy of history.

8

THE MEASURE OF
THE MAN

Müntzer was a driven and restless spirit seeking a faith that
would transform the world. Born into a time of radical changes,
he tried to come to grips with these changes as a theologian in a
church challenged by Luther's reforming movement. In his
quest for a faith that might withstand the pressure of history,
Müntzer studied furiously and read everything he could. He
often spent his last penny to acquire the latest editions of primary sources depicting the origins of Christendom as well as
books on ways to reform it. As a priest, he tried hard to be
involved in the lives of his people; and he tried even harder to
justify, through theological reflection, his priestly mission. It is
difficult to assess his thought and work because of the nomadic
quality of his life and a paucity of exact historical records. It is
equally difficult to clarify his relationship to other people and
other movements, be it to Luther or to the complex world of
late-medieval thought.

Nevertheless, there are sufficient sources to provide a basis for
an appraisal of Müntzer and for an assessment of his place in
history. Based on his own literary testimony, critical hindsight
warrants the thesis that he was the first Protestant theocrat. He
advocated the establishment of a society ruled by divine mandate alone, and he began with a "League of the Elect" in his
Allstedt parish in 1523, even though neither his league nor the
peasants' rebellion of 1524–25 fulfilled his theocratic expectations. It was left to the reformers Ulrich Zwingli and John Calvin
in Switzerland to realize in part what Müntzer had had in mind,

albeit without his emphasis on charismatic experience, his mystical visions, or his concept of holy war.

Müntzer's theocratic concept was grounded in the classic dialectic of the relationship between scriptural authority and charismatic experience, between the external Word and the internal experiencing of the Holy Spirit. The Word of Scripture, which Luther had elevated above the authority of the Roman Catholic magisterium, was for Müntzer the record of the earliest Christians driven by the Holy Spirit to bear witness to the unique lordship of Christ. Unlike Luther and other mainline reformers, however, Müntzer contended that the experiencing of the Holy Spirit was as powerful in postbiblical times as it had been at the time of the prophets and apostles. This focus on the timeless power of the Holy Spirit, this "spiritualism," was the controversial issue between Müntzer and the Wittenberg theologians. His theocratic spiritualism was the first manifestation of a Protestant "left wing" or "radical Reformation" embodied by groups like the Anabaptists and anti-Trinitarians.[1]

Müntzer, like Luther, stressed the value of internal turmoil *(Anfechtung)* as the critical mark of spiritual transformation. But he went further; to him such turmoil was the first step toward the victory of the spirit over flesh, purifying the soul from the selfish creaturely desires that prevent believers from establishing a theocratic society. He summarized his views rather well in the interpretation of Psalm 118 he wrote for his friend Christoph Meinhard in Eisleben in May of 1524. According to Müntzer, the experience of the psalm's author reflected the experience of all true believers. Internal struggle between spirit and flesh is what must occur before one can become an instrument of God's will.

1. For a typology of these various groups, see George H. Williams, *The Radical Reformation* (Philadelphia: Westminster Press, 1962). Williams describes Müntzer's "doctrine of Spirit-confirmed election" as having a "programmatically ecumenical character" because "inner suffering can go on in the soul of every man"—Christian, Turk, or pagan. Ibid., 56. That Müntzer was the leading spirit of the radical Reformation, including Anabaptism, and even influenced the ideas of Anglo-American "sects," is a thesis that can no longer be maintained in light of recent research. This thesis was suggested by Karl Holl, "Luther und die Schwärmer," *Gesammelte Aufsätze zur Kirchengeschichte*, 2 vols., 5th ed. (Tübingen: J. C. B. Mohr, 1927), 1:461–66. See the critical evaluation by Eric W. Gritsch, "Luther und die Schwärmer: Verworfene Anfechtung? Zum 50. Todesjahr Karl Holls," *Luther* 3 (1976): 105–21.

We must at every moment walk in the mortification of the flesh in such a way that our very name becomes a stench to the ungodly, for only someone who has been so tested can preach the name of God. And through the spirit of the fear of God—of which a true preacher is able to offer plenty of testimony—the hearers must first have heard Christ preached in their hearts.[2]

Müntzer likened this struggle to the experience of a fish in the sea:

When one becomes aware of one's origin in the wild water of one's encounter [with the Spirit of the fear of God] one must do like a fish that swims up and down in the roiling water: turn around, swimming with the current in order to reach one's starting point.... God's law is clear; it illumines the eyes of the elect and blinds the ungodly. It is faultless when the Spirit of the true fear of God is explained therein; and this happens when one dares to risk one's life for the truth.... God's righteousness must strangle our unbelief until we acknowledge that all lust is sin and that we have become hardened by our defense of lust.... Paul clearly taught this (2 Tim. 3[:2–5]).[3]

Müntzer's most persistent concern was the question of the origin and nature of one's relationship to God, the question of faith. In a letter from Allstedt, perhaps in 1524, to someone named Jeori who cannot be identified, he offered a more systematic answer than he had in the *Prague Manifesto*. According to him, everyone must experience the struggle between "simulated" faith originating with the institutional church and true faith given by the Holy Spirit.

Christ, the true Son of God, joins those who seem to be drowning and who lack all consolation. He does so at night, when one is most despondent, and the elect thinks He is a devil or a ghost. But He says, "O dearest, have no fear. It is I who have no other way to illumine you and to pour my grace into you." Then Peter, and the other elect, jump into the sea with Him [Matt. 14:29], eager to endure the flow. But the Gerasenes [inhabitants of the town of Gerasa, one of the cities in the Dekapolis, now in Jordan] demand that He move out of their land. They are the swine who drown in the water [Matt. 8:22], who refuse to learn about the coming of their faith, and who want to cover nature with nature. They use

2. MSB 402:16–21.
3. MSB 403:13–17,28–31;404:14–16,20–21.

Holy Scripture as they use fleshly things or pagan books. They do not tolerate the quick scribe who does not write with ink or other matter but with the engraving tool of His Spirit on the soul's abyss, so that He is recognized as the Son of God and the Christ who is the foremost of the sons of God.[4]

Certainty with regard to God's will, according to Müntzer, comes with *Anfechtung* and the start of faith in the human soul.

God's immutable will can be recognized only when one's own will has perished in broken-heartedness; and when that has been taken to heart, it is easy to tell how such a serious, suffering, diligent person feels. One does not believe in God because the whole world also believes, but because God has revealed and shown Himself through the order He has set in Himself and in all creatures. One must become aware of that and be certain of it, much more certain than about all natural things.... How can I know who is God or who is the devil, what is mine or what is not mine, unless I have escaped from myself? Oh what is the poverty of our spirit if we cannot speak of it because of our laziness! ... A simulated or imperfect faith causes offense. It must be eradicated without mercy, just as Christ [eradicated it in] His disciples when they had to suffer offense in His suffering.[5]

Müntzer was aware of the link between faith and ecstatic experience. As pastor in Allstedt, he collected, and probably tried to interpret, dreams parishioners reported to him. As he told Luther, "ecstasy and visions" were a measure of the grace Christ bestowed on individual believers, appropriate as long as they did not contradict the Word of God in Scripture.[6] But Müntzer viewed the believer's appropriation of the Word of God in the context of two elliptical foci, namely, the internal anxiety of one's conscience, produced by the purifying encounter with divine law, and the reception of the Holy Spirit directing one's soul and mind to the original, sinless state before God. In this sense, true believers become completely transformed, "become divine" *(vergottet)*, "formed like God and like Christ" *(gottförmig, christförmig)*.[7] His language echoed the cosmic Christology of

4. MSB 425:7–23.

5. MSB 425:29–38, 426:4–6, 7–8, 11–14.

6. That is Müntzer's interpretation to Luther of Eph. 4:7, contained in his letter from Allstedt. MSB 391:8–10.

7. MSB 281:28, 222:10, 11.

the Greek church fathers, some of whom Müntzer may have studied.[8] But Müntzer best expressed all these notions about the origin and nature of faith in his highly emotional style of preaching, the main channel of his witness. Even the lengthy treatises from the Allstedt period read more like homilies than systematic theological expositions.

Thus his spiritualism, which was anchored in the individual's experiencing of internal purification followed by reception of the Holy Spirit, was Müntzer's no to Luther and other reformers who maintained that faith comes through the external word, "through hearing" (Rom. 10:14). To Müntzer, such a position was the prattling of priests who had perverted the church shortly after the death of the apostles. Scripture, he asserted, at best attests to true faith; it does not produce it.

Müntzer defined a true believer as a person "overshadowed" by the Holy Spirit, lifted out of nothing into the "league of the elect" to become God's instrument.[9] As such, the elect must be separate from the established church and its political base, the world's princes. Müntzer wanted to lead these new-covenant people just as Elijah had led the true people of God against the prophets of Baal. This Elijah-like mission eventually linked Müntzer to the peasants' rebellion; he viewed it as the first step toward the liberation of the whole world from creaturely fleshly existence, and as the sign that God had initiated the final reformation—the restoration of the original human relationship with Him, as it had existed before the fall of Adam and Eve.

To Müntzer, those who refused to let the Holy Spirit do its

8. Müntzer's notes on the Latin church father Tertullian (MSB 539) have been analyzed by Wolfgang Ullmann, "Ordo rerum: Müntzers Randbemerkungen zu Tertullian als Quelle für das Verständnis seiner Theologie," *Theologische Versuche* 7 (Berlin: Evangelische Verlagsanstalt, 1976), 125–40. Müntzer also made two comments in a 1521 edition of the works of the Latin church father Cyprian, stressing the consensus of the common people regarding the election of church officials. Text and brief analysis in Bubenheimer, "Thomas Müntzers Wittenberger Studienzeit," 209–10.

9. Mary's experiencing of the Holy Spirit was to Müntzer an example of how one is re-created out of nothing. MSB 289:9–18. An attempt has been made to understand Müntzer on the basis of "verdict" *(Urteil)* and thus to see him as a "theologian of judgment" *(Gerichtstheologe)*, perhaps of the Last Judgment. But the argument is based on the doubtful assumption that the term "verdict" governs Müntzer's theology. See Gottfried Maron, "Thomas Müntzer als Theologe des Gerichts," ZKG 83 (1972): 195–225, esp. 223.

cleansing work in their sinful human souls would have to endure external punishment with the sword. Thus his quest for an invincible faith turned him into a charismatic preacher who claimed immediate access to the will of God. And his charismatic conviction made him a theocrat who felt commissioned to transform the old creation into a new heaven and a new world—if need be, with the sword of Gideon. He linked this understanding of faith as the expression of charismatic power to an apocalyptic vision of history. The "league of the elect" led by him, the new Daniel, would initiate a final "perfect and invincible reformation," and it would refuse to grant the right of life to those who rejected the offered personal, internal, spiritual transformation.[10]

Thus Müntzer did not envisage a "restitution of the apostolic church" or become a revolutionary in the classic Marxist sense.[11] Rather, he was committed to an apocalyptic vision of a society totally liberated from all earthly problems and return to the original order of creation before the Fall. He stated his vision clearly while in Allstedt, at the height of his success as a preacher, when he presented his interpretation of Luke 1: that the false and simulated faith of the worldly church would be supplanted by the true faith manifested in those whom God involved in the birth of Christ. Reminding his readers that Zachariah, Elizabeth, and Mary were the ones who received a faith founded upon belief in what seemed impossible by earthly standards, he wrote,

> The angel told the mother of God, "With God nothing is impossible" [Luke 1:37]. Why, my dearest friends? Truly, because it was something impossible, unthinkable, and unheard of (1 Cor. 2[:9], Isa. 64[:3–4]). All of us have to experience and to be reminded, at the advent of faith, that through the incarnation of Christ we fleshly, earthly people should become gods and thus disciples with

10. MSB 255:24–25, 257:19.

11. E, 3, based on evidence from the Prague Manifesto of 1521, proffers the thesis that Müntzer tried to restitute the apostolic church. But Müntzer had progressed from that notion to his radical apocalyptic vision in Allstedt a few years later. What makes Marxist historiography problematic is its assumption that nineteenth-century categories of radical social change and "revolution" can be applied to Müntzer, who was not a revolutionary in that sense. See Bensing, *Thomas Müntzer*, 92, where his legacy is summarized in the words of a socialist playwright.

Him, taught by Him and made divine *(vergottet)*. Indeed, much more than that, [we should] be completely transformed in Him, so that earthly life swings into heaven (Phil. 3[:20–21]).[12]

There is no doubt that Müntzer combined his theological reflections with pragmatic pastoral concern for those who were victims—peasants, miners, weavers, and others who were caught in the sixteenth-century feudal system. Luther never recognized this dimension of Müntzer's work. To him, Müntzer was a satanic prophet whose vision and program must be suppressed. Müntzer respected Luther as a genuine reformer when they met during Müntzer's earlier years. But in the end, Luther was to Müntzer the satanic defender of the status quo, who marshaled the opposition of political tyrants to changes Müntzer advocated. They reduced each other to convenient targets of demonization. But the plight of the peasants and other victims of the feudal system was real, and Müntzer experienced it firsthand in Zwickau, Allstedt, and on his journeys to southern Germany and Switzerland.

As a gifted orator and well-educated priest, Müntzer created his own language and slogans with which he hoped to persuade the common people, as well as the intelligentsia, to join him in a common cause. His language bristles with terminology echoing German mystics, Joachim of Fiore, and the Hussites. This has caused scholars to search for possible sources of his thought; they have arrived at a variety of answers. One could easily succumb to the historiographical temptation of classifying him as merely a representative of specific ideas or movements that impacted on him—a method known as *Wirkungsgeschichte*, often linked to *Entstehungsgeschichte*, the history of origins. At this point Leif Grane's sage warning should be heeded: if structures of thought are made the starting point of historical analysis, a historical person is transformed into a type, disclosing a particular structure or thought rather than historical reality.[13]

---

12. MSB 281:12–32.

13. An observation made concerning the work of Hans-Jürgen Goertz, *Innere und äussere Ordnung in der Theologie Thomas Müntzers*. See Leif Grane, "Thomas Müntzer und Martin Luther" in *Bauernkriegs-Studien*, ed. Bernd Moeller, Schriften des Vereins für Reformationsgeschichte 189 (Gütersloh, W. Ger.: Gerd Mohn, 1975), 71.

One can only be grateful for the careful and manifold studies, whether or not the conclusions—that he was a Luther disciple, a late-medieval German mystic, a Taborite or Joachimite apocalypticist, or a combination of all of these—hold true.

One must also grant Müntzer his own, perhaps odd individuality, which may have been forged by his passionate quest for an invincible faith and a brave new world. In his literary torso and in the reaction of those who heard him preach, one senses in Müntzer a singular passion to overcome the cruel divisions of a Christian world and to reach out, at least in a visionary sense, for something better—for something that might conform to what God had in mind for his creation. His vision, when judged by historical realism, makes him seem a Utopian idealist. Yet the world has never existed without idealists who yearn for the unity of a humankind governed by the will of God. Müntzer could foresee the unity of Christians, Jews, and pagans, all made equal on the basis of an internal, individual purification, and all rising up against a world ruled by an idolatry that refused to let God be God. This was his impossible dream.

It was his encounter with idolatry and tyranny that frustrated Müntzer, infuriated him, and ultimately made him "unreasonable." He may, in his final days, have become a wayward witness violating the religious and cultural orthodoxy of his time. But perhaps he became what he was because he encountered nothing but prejudice and hatred on the part of the ecclesiastical and political establishment in Saxony and elsewhere. His witness is a reminder to Christians of how important it is, in the face of God, who is the final judge in all matters, that they be more tolerant with each other than is usually the case.

9

MÜNTZERIANA

"Whoever has seen Müntzer may say that he has seen the devil himself in his greatest wrath." So wrote Luther, three days after Müntzer's death.[1] He soon afterward popularized his demonization of Müntzer in the treatise. *A Terrible Story and Judgment of God About Thomas Müntzer, In Which God Publicly Gives the Lie to This Same Spirit and Condemns Him.*[2] Appealing to the existing climate of superstition, Luther declared that Müntzer's execution was a warning to those who still contemplated rebellion. If God had spoken through Müntzer, he contended, this *Schwärmer* would not have ended the way he did. He concluded by declaring that Müntzer had to die because he was too boastful about his relationship with God. "Since Thomas has failed, it is quite clear that he used God's name but spoke and acted in the name of the devil."[3]

Müntzer's "enthusiasm," his "swarming" *(Schwärmerei)* as Luther called it, had stung Luther to the degree that he developed an allergy to anything associated with Müntzer's name. Even in his last sermon, on February 15, 1546—twenty-one years after Müntzer's death—Luther belittled Müntzer as another "Master Wiseacre *(Meister Klügling)* who, like the pope, impeded the gospel's course by trying to dominate it with his own wisdom."[4]

1. Letter to Rühel, May 30, 1525. WA.BR 3:525, 28—516, 35.
2. *Eine Schreckliche Geschichte und Gericht Gottes über Thomas Müntzer . . .* WA 18:362–74.
3. WA 18:367.16–17.
4. WA 51:188.24; 189.39—190.2. LW 51:386–87.

Another pamphlet, *The History of Thomas Müntzer, the Origi-
nator of the Thuringian Rebellions, Very Useful to Read*, appeared
shortly after Luther's account.[5] Possibly written by Philip Melanchthon, Luther's "pussyfooting" friend, it delineated what
was to become the typical version of the Protestant Müntzer
legend: Since the devil always tries to destroy the pure gospel,
he possessed Müntzer in an attempt to destroy Luther's sowing
of the Word of God; Müntzer was so possessed that he went far
beyond the devil's original plan and advocated the violent removal of all political authorities; but then he tried to cover up
his satanic teaching by claiming that he had received it directly
from God. The pamphlet likened Müntzer to the ancient here-
siarch Mani (ca. 216–276) who had advocated a radical distinction between a world of light and one of darkness as manifested
in the "elect" of God and the servants of evil.

Thus Müntzer was portrayed as one of the great misfits of the
history of salvation, a German example of how the forces of evil
threaten divinely established government. "Examples like these
should be remembered by posterity and should be written down
diligently as special stories about God."[6]

One of the immediate results of this kind of propaganda was
that Protestant historians made of Müntzer the symbol of dissent and heresy. Disciples of Luther began to associate Müntzer
with the Anabaptist sect; when radical Anabaptists succeeded in
winning the Westphalian city of Münster to their cause, Protestant and Catholic princes launched a crusade against them in
1535 and annihilated most of them. Soon "Münster" and
"Müntzer" became interchangeable slogans used by defenders
of Protestant orthodoxy to show that Anabaptists exhibited a
demonic spirit. Even the tolerant German Pietists accepted this
view. Gottfried Arnold's popular *Nonpartisan History of the
Church and Its Heresies from the Beginning of the New Testament
Until the Year of Christ 1688*—though granting Müntzer "the
spirit of God" at the beginning—concluded that Satan in the end
tricked him away from "God's gentle leadership."[7]

    5. *Die Historia Thomae Müntzers, des Anfängers der thüringischen Aufruhr, sehr
nützlich zu lesen.* St.L. 16:160–73.

    6. Ibid., 173.

    7. Arnold, *Unpartheiische Kirchen-und Ketzerhistorie vom Anfang des Neuen
Testaments bis auf das Jahr Christi 1688* (1729; reprint, Hildesheim: Olms, 1967),
466, 468.

Leopold von Ranke, the author of the first "scientific" history of the Reformation, also adhered to the original Müntzer legend. He labelled Müntzer and the Anabaptists "too confused" to make a contribution to "the great world-historical march of culture."[8]

Whereas the Protestant version of the Müntzer legend attempts to disassociate Müntzer from Luther, the Roman Catholic version is characterized by a clear desire to portray him as the embodiment of radicalized Lutheranism. The Dominican biographer John Cochlaeus blamed Luther for the violence and destruction caused by the peasants in 1525, stating that Luther's "associates" had simply carried out what he had preached.[9] Later Catholic historians like Hartmann Grisar suggested that Luther rejected Müntzer because he was viewed as a rival leader in the movement.[10] The rather tolerant historian Joseph Lortz saw Müntzer as "an important manifestation of religious subjectivism" which Luther had advocated.[11]

Both the heirs and the enemies of the Reformation tried to expel Müntzer from their religious traditions, but the early Marxist-Socialist-Communist movement adopted him as a forerunner of the Marxist cause. In the wake of the 1848 revolution, Frederick Engels reinterpreted what he called the German Peasants' War of 1525 as an event pointing to the final emancipation of the oppressed classes of society. "His [Müntzer's] political doctrine extended as far beyond the existing social and political conditions as his theology surpassed the ideas valid for his time."[12] Basing his conclusions on the historical research on the peasants' rebellion done by William Zimmermann, a Protestant pastor who supported the 1848 revolution, Engels declared that

8. Leopold von Ranke, *Deutsche Geschichte im Zeitalter der Reformation*, 7th ed., 6 vols. (Leipzig: Dunker and Humblot, 1894), 2:152; 5:345.

9. In a commentary to Luther's treatise *Against the Robbing and Murdering Hordes of Peasants* 1525 (WA 18:357–61. LW 46:49–55), quoted in Adolf Herte, *Die Lutherkommentare des Johannes Cochlaeus*, Religionsgeschichtliche Studien und Texte 33 (Münster: Aschendorff, 1935), 177.

10. Grisar, *Luther*, trans. E. M. Lamond, 6 vols. (St. Louis: Herder & Herder; London: Kegan Paul, Trench, Truebner, 1914–17), 3:4.

11. Josef Lortz, *The Reformation in Germany*, trans. Ronald Hals, 2 vols. (New York and London: Herder, 1968), 1:356.

12. Friedrich Engels, *Der deutsche Bauernkrieg* (Berlin: Vorwärts, 1920), 54. This edition is based on Engels's final revision of 1875.

Müntzer had failed because the historical conditions were "not yet ripe" for a realization of his ideals since these conditions were still trapped in religion.[13] Later Marxists, however—notably the Germans Karl Kautsky and Ernst Bloch—insisted that Communism had been anticipated in Müntzer's religious visions. Bloch contended that the old struggle with God manifested in the Taborite, Joachimite, and Communist type of radical Anabaptism recurred in the Bolshevik realization of Marxism; and that Müntzer's view of history was its prelude.[14]

A sophisticated version of the Marxist Müntzer legend was produced by the Russian historian M. M. Smirin, who depicted Müntzer as the leader of a "folk-reformation" *(Volksreformation)* as opposed to Luther's "princes-reformation" *(Fürstenreformation).* Smirin defended the thesis that "the folk reformation of the sixteenth century received its final form and theoretical expression in Müntzer's teaching," but the sociopolitical aims of the peasants' rebellion were confused by religion. "Marx characterized it in the brief formula: 'the Peasants' War, the most significant fact of German history, was wrecked by theology.' "[15]

The creators and propagators of the Müntzer legend did not bother to search for Müntzer's writings, which Duke George of Saxony and Landgrave Philip of Hesse had deposited in the archives of Weimar, Dresden, and Marburg shortly after Müntzer's execution. George of Saxony had taken a sackful of writings from Müntzer's widow, probably wanting them as curiosity items for his ducal collections in Dresden and Weimar; Philip of Hesse had come into possession of a batch of letters and stored them in the library of the University of Marburg, which he founded in 1527. It was a rural Saxon pastor, John K. Seidemann, who discovered these writings in the archives in 1842, and added forty-seven items of original Müntzer writings

13. Ibid., 105–6.

14. Ernst Bloch, *Thomas Müntzer als Theologe der Revolution,* Bibliothek Suhrkamp 77 (Berlin: Suhrkamp, 1962 [1st ed., 1921]), 108. His historiographical "misunderstanding" has been analyzed by Iris Geyer, *Thomas Müntzer im Bauernkrieg* (Bensigheim: Verlag K.H.V., 1982), 41–52. See also Karl Kautsky, *Communism in Central Europe in the Time of the Reformation,* trans. J. L. and E. G. Muliken (New York: Russell and Russell, 1959 [1st ed., 1920]), chap. 4.

15. Smirin, op. cit., 646, 648.

in an appendix to the biography he published.[16] Carl E. Förstemann edited *Documents Concerning the History of Thomas
Muentzer and the Peasants' War in Thuringia 1523–1525* at about
the same time.[17] The Saxon and Thüringian Commissions for
History and Archeology soon commissioned additional special
studies. The final phase of Müntzer's life became the subject of
the first major critical work done by Otto Merx, a young
Lutheran historian.[18]

Finally, the founder of modern Luther research, Karl Holl,
offered a critical assessment of Müntzer based on an analysis of
existing primary sources. "I take him more seriously," Holl
wrote in his now famous 1922 essay "Luther and the
Schwärmer," "than is otherwise customary in the history of the
church."[19] Holl analyzed Müntzer's teaching and placed it into
the context of a broad interpretation of what was later called
"the radical Reformation" or "left wing of the Reformation."
According to Holl, the "radical Reformation" helped shape Anglo-American Christianity. Still, to Holl it was Luther who was
the reformer "who presented the creative religious truth."
Luther's appreciation of "the *community* in a nation" is, in Holl's
judgment, "closer to Christianity than the idea of one who val-
ues 'freedom' above anything else," as does Anglo-Ameri-
canism.[20]

Heinrich Boehmer, a young scholar from Zwickau, continued
the quest for the historical Müntzer as based on his writings,
and he labelled Müntzer a "spiritualist" who had little, if anything, in common with the Müntzer the Communists had presented.[21] In 1931, Annemarie Lohmann, one of Boehmer's students, did a study of Müntzer's intellectual development and
concluded that he was full of inconsistencies.[22] Ernst Troeltsch,

16. Seidemann, *Thomas Müntzer.*
17. They are contained in Förstemann, *Neues Urkundenbuch.*
18. Otto Merx, *Müntzer und Pfeiffer.*
19. Holl, *Gesammelte Aufsätze* 1:425.
20. Ibid., 467.
21. Heinrich Boehmer, "Thomas Müntzer und das jüngste Deutschland,"
Gesammelte Aufsätze (Gotha: Flamberg, 1927), 187–222.
22. Lohmann, *Zur geistigen Entwicklung Thomas Müntzers.*

the author of the monumental work *The Social Teaching of the Christian Churches* made the judgment that Müntzer "is the first instance of a pronounced opposition to the Protestant church type" as over against the "sect type" that represents "the ethics of spiritual religion."[23]

By 1933, Heinrich Boehmer, Paul Kirn, and Otto H. Brandt published editions of Müntzer's correspondence and other selected documents dealing with the peasants' rebellion;[24] Carl Hinrichs edited Müntzer's political writings in 1950;[25] and the Society for Reformation History crowned the effort of these scholars with what purports to be a complete text-critical edition of Müntzer's works.[26] Müntzer's literary output, however, poses severe research problems: his German is hard to translate, since it predates commonly accepted grammatical structures; there are significant omissions in the texts; and Müntzer's handwriting is extremely difficult to decipher.

There are extensive biographical problems also: little is known about Müntzer's early years; the year of his birth has to be guessed at on the basis of meager evidence, such as immatriculation records and the date a prebend was bestowed on him after his ordination. A "Thomas Montzer" and the names of other young men appear in the records of the Stolberg City Council in 1484 as having paid a fine for being rowdy *(ungebärdig)* in a dance hall. This discovery led some to conclude that "Montzer" was "Müntzer," who must have been at least sixteen to attend a dance hall, which would make him at least fifty-seven or fifty-eight at the time of his execution, therefore born in 1467 or 1468.[27] The emerging consensus is that his birth year should

---

23. Troeltsch, *The Social Teaching of the Christian Churches*, trans. Olive Wyon, 2 vols. (New York: Macmillan, 1931 [original German ed., 1912]), 1:754.

24. Boehmer and Kirn, *Thomas Müntzers Briefwechsel*. Otto H. Brandt, *Thomas Müntzer: Sein Leben und seine Schriften* (Jena: Diederichs, 1933).

25. Carl Hinrichs, ed., *Thomas Müntzer: die politischen Schriften mit Kommentar*, Hallesche Monographien 17 (Halle: Niemeyer, 1950).

26. MSB.

27. See Hermann Goebke, "Neue Forschungen über Thomas Müntzer bis zum Jahre 1520," HZ 9 (1957): 1–30, esp. 3–4. Goebke also surmised that Müntzer, like Luther, was an Augustinian monk. This was thoroughly refuted by Adolar Zumkeller, "Thomas Müntzer—Augustiner?" *Augustiniana* 9 (1959): 380–85. Goebke's method and conclusions have also been severely criticized by other Marxist historians. See especially Manfred Bensing, "Thomas Müntzers Frühzeit," ZGW 14 (1966): 423–30.

be set before 1491, because Canon Law required a candidate to have attained his twenty-fourth birthday before he could be ordained. If one assumes that Müntzer was ordained shortly before he received a prebend from St. Michael's in Braunschweig in 1514, one could assume his birth year to be 1489.[28] Some historians favor the year 1488–89 because they assume that the "Thomas Müntzer of Quedlinburg" mentioned in the 1506 immatriculation list at the University of Leipzig was indeed *the* Thomas Müntzer, since the university required that students be seventeen when starting their baccalaureate studies.[29] Difficulties are compounded by the fact that the name "Müntzer" is spelled in a variety of ways in various sources: Müntczer, Munzer, and Muntzer by Müntzer himself; Montzer, and Münther in Low German. The name refers to the vocation of mining, thus increasing speculations about Thomas's early life.[30] Since the evidence existing for the period before 1517 is mostly circumstantial, a reconstruction of Müntzer's early years is at best hypothetical.

An assessment of Müntzer's relationship to Luther is equally difficult, since Müntzer soon went his own way, although he may have been in Luther's orbit during his early career. The complexity of the question becomes apparent in Walter Elliger's summary of that relationship: Müntzer was Luther's disciple "who, to be sure, already came to Wittenberg with the bias of an

28. For an assessment of the controversial data regarding the year of birth, see Siegfried Bräuer, "Zu Müntzers Geburtsjahr," LJ 36 (1969): 80–83. Calculations range from 1467 to 1493. See Marianne Schaub, *Müntzer contre Luther. Le droit divin contre l'absolutisme princier* (Paris: Centre National des Lettres, 1984), 37. See also the analysis of old and new data by Ulrich Bubenheimer, "Thomas Müntzer und der Anfang," 1–30, esp. 19–20. Analysis and text of the prebend presentation to Müntzer in Bubenheimer, "Thomas Müntzer in Braunschweig," Part 1, 37, 66 (1.4). On consensus regarding the year of birth "before 1491," see Bubenheimer, "Thomas Müntzer und der Anfang," 19.

29. E, 17. Georg Erler, ed., *Die Matrikel der Universität Leipzig*, Codex Diplomaticus Saxoniae Regiae 16, 3 vols. (Leipzig, 1895–1902), 1:477. See also Heinrich Boehmer, *Studien zu Thomas Müntzer* (Leipzig: Edelmann, 1922), 12.

30. E, 11, for example, follows Goebke's hypothetical conclusions, and assumes that Matthias Montzer was Müntzer's father. Goebke himself thought that this same Montzer was Müntzer's uncle (op. cit., 9–10, n. 3). Schaub (op. cit., 37) used a "Karl Münter" from Goebke's genealogical charts to surmise that Müntzer's father was a Stolberg "rope-maker" (*Seilermeister*, Goebke, op. cit., 7–8, 11–13). See the critical analysis of the data in Bubenheimer, "Thomas Müntzer in Braunschweig," Part 2, 79–81.

independent and personal formulation of questions *(Fragestellung)*, and heard and assimilated the 'new teaching' of the 'young Luther' in this context. . . . Luther made the radical break, not Müntzer, even though it was he [Müntzer] who had already separated himself from him [Luther]."[31] The most recent Marxist biography calls Müntzer an "ally" *(Bundesgenosse)* who supported and admired Luther without, however, ever having become dependent on him.[32] Thomas Nipperdey contends that Luther was Müntzer's "basic theological problem" *(Grundproblem)* because Müntzer turned Luther's theology upside down, as it were, focusing on the subjective experiencing of the Holy Spirit rather than on the authority of the external word.[33] Bernhard Lohse refutes this view, and, on the basis of the influence of late medieval German mysticism on Müntzer, calls attention to Müntzer's independence from Luther.[34] Ulrich Bubenheimer thinks that Müntzer developed his views, especially his anti–Roman Catholic positions, without any help from Luther because he had been a successful theological critic of indulgences in Braunschweig before Luther's Ninety-Five Theses appeared in 1517. But Bubenheimer arrives at such a conclusion on the basis of an investigation of Müntzer's "social interlacing" *(soziale Verflechtungen)*, a rather controversial research method, and relies heavily on a source that calls Müntzer a "persecutor of injustice."[35]

In addition to the unresolved issues of Müntzer's social origins and his relationship to Luther, there is also the question of Müntzer's dependence on late medieval ideas, such as mysticism. The most recent German biographical sketches of

31. E, 7.

32. Bensing, *Thomas Müntzer,* 30.

33. Thomas Nipperdey, "Theologie und Revolution bei Thomas Müntzer," ARG 54 (1963): 40, 47, 83–84.

34. Bernhard Lohse, "Luther und Müntzer," *Luther* (1974): 12–32, esp. 17, 31–32. See Eric W. Gritsch, "Thomas Müntzer and Luther: A Tragedy of Errors" in *Radical Tendencies in the Reformation. Divergent Perspectives,* ed. Hans J. Hillerbrand (Sixteenth Century Essays and Studies 9, Kirksville: Sixteenth Century Journal Publishers, 1988), 55–83.

35. Bubenheimer, "Thomas Müntzer" in *Protestantische Profile,* ed. Klaus Scholder and Dieter Kleinmann (Königstein, Ts.: Athenäum, 1983), 36–37. See also his essays "Thomas Müntzer in Braunschweig," Pts. 1—2. On the research method, 2, 79. On Müntzer's title, Scholder and Kleinmann, 36–37.

Müntzer tend to ascribe more significance to the influence on him of late medieval German mystics like John Tauler (ca. 1300–61). According to Siegfried Bräuer and Hans Jürgen Goertz, the "first beginnings" *(Ansatz)* of Müntzer's "theology of revolution" can be traced to "grades of tradition" *(Traditionsgefälle)* in medieval mysticism; to the apocalyptic milieu created by Joachimite eschatological speculations and by Taborite (Hussite) millennialism; and to the early writings of Luther, "in the way Müntzer understood them." But both authors explain that Müntzer's thoughts were "erratic" *(sprunghaft)* and "associative"; that the sources of his piety and argumentation can rarely be ascertained; and that the motives for his actions are not always clear.[36]

In 1967, Hans Jürgen Goertz attempted to show that Müntzer's views are totally grounded in medieval mysticism and in its dialectic of internal and external order.[37] According to Goertz, Müntzer used the mystical thought form "the order of God" to dedicate his life to restituting this original unity, lost through human sin, between God and the human soul. Once the "inner order" is restored in the believer, the world's "external order" can be transformed into an appropriate covenant of obedience to God, and a cadre of the elect, organized by Müntzer and poised to attack the sinful external structures of the world, will accomplish this transformation—thus the link between theology and revolution. This systematic argumentation is attractive. But Goertz attempts to find a leitmotif by which one can reconstruct the "live" Müntzer, and Müntzer's structure of thought is too complex, indeed contradictory at times, to warrant such neat conclusions.

Moreover, it can also be argued that Müntzer was as much influenced by Hussite-Taborite millennialist ideas as he was by mysticism or its Neo-Platonic philosophical context.[38] Such a

36. "Thomas Müntzer," 347.

37. Goertz, *Innere und aussere Ordnung,* esp. 25–28. English summary in Goertz and Walter Klassen, eds., *Profiles of Radical Reformers. Biographical Sketches from Thomas Müntzer to Paracelsus* (Scottdale, Pa.; Kitchener, Ontario: Herald, 1982), 29–44. Goertz modified his thesis in "Der Mystiker mit dem Hammer," KD 20 (1974): 23–53.

38. See Reinhard Schwarz, *Die apokalyptische Theologie Thomas Müntzers und der Taboriten,* Beiträge zur historischen Theologie 55 (Tübingen: J. C. B. Mohr, 1977), 125–26.

link is possible because Müntzer stayed in Prague for a while and spoke positively of John Hus. Smirin tried to show Müntzer's dependence on the German mystical and on the Hussite traditions as well as on the philosophy of history presented by Joachim of Fiore.[39] In a comparison between Müntzer's and Luther's views on faith, it was suggested that Müntzer had revived the old conflict between Platonists and Aristotelians because he rejected normative externals and thus echoed the medieval quarrel between "realists" and "conceptionalists."[40] A more cautious interpretation is offered by Stephen E. Ozment, who asserted that Müntzer's "theology of the heart" becomes a revolutionary ideology when applied to society, but that "there is much controversy on this relationship."[41] Thus there is much that remains unclear about Müntzer's early life, about his relationship to Luther, and about his affinity to or dependence on medieval thought.

The quest for the historical Müntzer and the questions concerning the origins and the impact of his ideas *(Entstehungs-Wirkungsgeschichte)* have produced a research labyrinth that steadily increases in complexity.[42] But Protestant, Roman Catholic, and Marxist historians have begun to cooperate in their search for the real Müntzer. Since most of Müntzer's activities took place in what is now the GDR, he has become the hero of the sixteenth-century Reformation there, in contrast to Luther, who is perceived to have been less "revolutionary" than Müntzer.[43] His portrait has appeared on banknotes and stamps;

39. Op. cit., chaps. 2–4.

40. See Helmar Junghans, "Ursachen für das Glaubensverständnis Thomas Müntzers 1524" in *Der deutsche Bauernkrieg und Thomas Müntzer*, ed. Max Steinmetz (Leipzig: Karl Marx Universität, 1976), 148–49.

41. *Mysticism and Dissent. Religious Ideology and Social Protest in the Sixteenth Century* (New Haven and London: Yale University Press, 1973), 91 and n. 109.

42. See the evaluation of Müntzer texts and research in Siegfried Bräuer, "Müntzerforschung von 1965 bis 1975," LJ 44 (1977): 127–41; 45 (1978): 102–39. Also Hans J. Hillerbrand, *Thomas Müntzer: A Bibliography*, Bulletin of the Library of the Foundation for Reformation Research 4 (St. Louis: 1976). For a Marxist evaluation of Müntzer research, see Max Steinmetz, "Thomas Müntzer in der Forschung der Gegenwart," ZGW 23 (1975): 665–85.

43. "Theses Concerning Martin Luther," *The Luther Quincentenary in the German Democratic Republic 1983* (Panorama DDR, Auslandspresseagentur, Berlin), esp. p. 17. The theses were written by scholars drawn from universities and the Academy of Sciences, chaired by Horst Bartel, Director of the Academy's Historical Institute.

plays about him have been written and performed; streets have been named after him. Both Müntzer and the peasants' rebellion have become vital components of the high-school curricula in the socialist countries of Europe, where students learn about "world-historical aspects" of Müntzer's "revolution."[44]

The GDR "theses" on the occasion of Müntzer's five-hundredth birthday in 1989 are linked to the fortieth anniversary of the GDR.

> [The GDR] also honors, along with Thomas Müntzer, all other figures and fighters of the early bourgeois revolution initiated by Martin Luther, and in this way links up with the honors [paid] on the occasions of the four-hundred-fiftieth anniversary of the Reformation in 1967, of the four-hundred-fiftieth anniversary in 1975 of the German peasants' war [and] the death of Thomas Müntzer, and of the five-hundredth birthday of Martin Luther.[45]

Müntzer is perceived as the forerunner of the French and other revolutions, since he advocated "that the power should be given to the common people."[46] Thus "both Luther and Müntzer are solidly anchored in those traditions to which the GDR feels itself obligated."[47]

Müntzer's nomadic life, his radical ideas, and his violent death have all inspired playwrights both in the sixteenth century and afterward. In 1565, his ideas were used for the first time in a play in Brandenburg, the setting of which was a "devil's council" with Satan presenting an account of his work, including the creation of a rebellion on the basis of Müntzer's notion of the authority of the local congregation.[48] In a play produced for the schools in Thuringia in 1572, Müntzer appears as the preacher who calls for the peasants' rebellion and is

44. See the survey of textbooks on history in Socialist countries in Dieter Schiewe, "Zur Darstellung Thomas Müntzers in vergleichbaren Geschichts-lehrbüchern sozialistischer Länder" in *Der deutsche Bauernkrieg und Thomas Müntzer,* ed. Max Steinmetz (Leipzig: Karl Marx Universität, 1976), 291–97.

45. "Thesen über Thomas Müntzer. Zum 500. Geburtstag," *Sonderdruck aus der ZGW* 36 (1988): 99.

46. Müntzer's letter to the people of Eisenach, dated May 9, 1525. MSB 463:11–12.

47. "Thesen," 121.

48. See Siegfried Bräuer, "Thomas Müntzer im Schauspiel des 16. Jahrhunderts" in Steinmetz, *Der deutsche Bauernkrieg,* 112.

executed for sedition; but he is not characterized as diabolical.[49] In 1970, Dieter Forte, associated with West German television and the Basel Theater, wrote a play entitled *Martin Luther and Thomas Müntzer, or the Introduction of Bookkeeping*, which premiered in Basel in December of that year.[50] In this play Müntzer appears as an advocate of humanity in the face of medieval feudalistic capitalism as represented by the Fugger Bank in Augsburg and by Luther and Philip Melanchthon. Forte did not make Müntzer a hero, but rather portrayed the impact of two revolutions of the early sixteenth century: the invention of the printing press and the peasants' rebellion.

Müntzer's literary legacy consists of a torso bequeathed to the world by his enemies: about fifty letters, six treatises, one confession, a so-called recantation, various fragments, and some liturgical writings that constitute the first non–Roman Catholic reform of worship in Germany—all in all, about five hundred fifty pages in print.[51] No details of Müntzer's physical appearance have been preserved, presumably because he was said to have been an incarnation of the devil.[52]

The British church historian E. Gordon Rupp presented Müntzer to the modern world as a victim of what could be called a tragedy of errors.

> In him, as in almost no other figure, we come near to that smothered medieval undercurrent of injustice, resentment, and pain, now defeated once more, now driven dangerously underground—a tradition lost to the church but one day to return to the gates of Christendom—aggressive, heretical, anticlerical, yet a wit-

49. Ibid., 115–21.

50. *Martin Luther und Thomas Müntzer oder die Einführung der Buchhaltung* (Berlin: Wagenbach, 1971).

51. MSB. English translation by Peter Matheson, *The Collected Works of Thomas Müntzer* (Edinburgh: T. & T. Clark, 1988). Ulrich Bubenheimer has discovered some Müntzer fragments in Wittenberg ("Thomas Müntzers Nachschrift einer Wittenberger Hieronymusvorlesung") and might discover more. Teams of scholars from the GDR and the Federal Republic of Germany are editing what now exists.

52. There are several pictures of Müntzer, but none can claim to be an exact portrait. Christoph of Sichem, a Dutch artist, is the creator of the most popular one. It was published in 1608 in a collection depicting the major heretics of Christianity. For an evaluation of the various pictures, see Günther Franz, "Die Bildnisse Thomas Müntzers" *Archiv Für Kulturgeschichte* 25 (1935): 21–37.

ness somewhere to a Christian failure of practical compassion. Thomas Müntzer, like the Iron Curtain, should give us an uneasy conscience.[53]

53. E. Gordon Rupp, "Luther and Thomas Müntzer (1491–1525)" in *Luther Today*, vol. 1 of *The Martin Luther Lectures*, 5 vols., ed. Roland H. Bainton et al. (Decorah, Iowa: Luther College Press, 1957), 146. Part of a broadcast to East Germany in 1956, transmitted to Moscow through the British Broadcasting Company.

BIBLIOGRAPHY

THOMAS MÜNTZER'S WORKS

Franz, Günther, ed. *Thomas Müntzer, Schriften und Briefe. Kritische Gesamtausgabe.* (Quellen und Forschungen zur Reformationsgeschichte 33). Gütersloh, W. Ger.: Gerd Mohn, 1968.

Matheson, Peter, trans. *The Collected Works of Thomas Müntzer.* Edinburgh: T. & T. Clark, 1988.

OTHER SOURCES*

*in addition to those cited in the list of abbreviations:

Arnold, Gottfried. *Unpartheiische Kirchen-und Ketzerhistorie vom Anfang des Neuen Testaments biss auff das Jahr Christi 1688.* 2 vols. 1729. Reprint. Hildesheim: Olms, 1967.

Bailey, Richard. "The Sixteenth Century Apocalyptic Heritage and Thomas Müntzer." *The Mennonite Quarterly Review* 57 (1983): 27–44.

Baylor, Michael G. "Thomas Müntzer's First Publication." *The Sixteenth Century Journal* 17 (1986): 451–58.

Bender, Harold S. "The Zwickau Prophets, Thomas Müntzer, and the Anabaptists." *The Mennonite Quarterly Review* 27 (1953): 3–16.

Bensing, Manfred. "Idee und Praxis des 'christlichen Verbündnisses' bei Thomas Müntzer." *Wissenschaftliche Zeitschrift der Karl Marx Universität Leipzig* 14 (1965): 459–71.

———. *Thomas Müntzer.* 3d ed., rev. Leipzig: VEB Bibliographisches Institut, 1983.

———. "Thomas Müntzer und Nordhausen (Harz) 1522." *Zeitschrift für Geschichtswissenshaft* 10 (1962): 1095–1123.

———. "Thomas Müntzer und die Reformationsbewegung in Nordhausen 1522 bis 1525." *Beiträge zur Heimatkunde aus Stadt und Kreis Nordhausen.* Nordhausen: Meyenburg Museum, 1983, Heft 8:4–18.

———. *Thomas Müntzer und der Thüringer Aufstand 1525.* Berlin: Deutscher Verlag der Wissenschaften, 1966.

———. "Thomas Müntzers Aufenthalt in Nordhausen 1522— Zwischenspiel oder Zeit der Entscheidung?" *Harz-Zeitschrift* 19–20 (1967–68): 35–62.

———. "Thomas Müntzers Früzeit. Zu Hermann Goebke's 'Neue Forschungen über Thomas Müntzer.'" *Zeitschrift für Geschichtswissenschaft* 14 (1966): 423–30.

———. *Thomas Müntzers Kampf und Weggefährten. Veröffentlichungen der Bauernkriegsgedenkstätte "Panorama."* Bad Frankenhausen, Heft 1, 1977.

Bensing, Manfred, and Winfried Trillitzsch. "Bernhard Dappens 'Articuli … contra Lutheranos.' Zur Auseinandersetzung der Jüterboger Franziskaner mit Thomas Müntzer und Franz Günther 1519." *Zeitschrift für Geschichtswissenschaft* 14 (1967): 113–47.

Blickle, Peter. *The Revolution of 1525. The German Peasants War from a New Perspective.* Trans. T. A. Bradey, Jr. Baltimore: Johns Hopkins University Press, 1981.

Bloch, Ernst. *Thomas Müntzer als Theologe der Revolution.* 1921. Reprint. Bibliothek Suhrkamp 77. Berlin: Aufbau Verlag, 1962.

Boehmer, Heinrich. *Studien zu Thomas Müntzer.* Leipzig: Alexander Edelmann, 1922.

———. "Thomas Müntzer und das jüngste Deutschland." *Gesammelte Aufsätze.* Gotha: Flamberg Verlag, 1927, 187–222.

Boehmer, Heinrich, and Kirn, Paul, eds. *Thomas Müntzers Briefwechsel. Auf Grund der Handschriften und ältesten Vorlagen.* Schriften der sächsischen Kommission für Geschichte 34. Leipzig, E. Ger.: B. G. Teubner, 1931.

Brandt, Otto H. *Thomas Müntzer: Sein Leben und seine Schriften.* Jena: Diederichs, 1933.

Bräuer, Siegfried. "Die erste Gesamtausgabe von Thomas Müntzers Schriften und Briefe," *Luther-Jahrbuch* 38 (1971): 121–31.

———. "Müntzerforschung von 1965 bis 1975." *Luther-Jahrbuch* 44 (1977): 127–41, 45 (1978): 102–39.

———. "Thomas Müntzer." *Zeichen der Zeit* 29 (1975): 121–29.

———. "Thomas Müntzer im Schauspiel des 16. Jahrhunderts." In *Der deutsche Bauernkrieg und Thomas Müntzer,* ed. Max Steinmetz, 112–21. Leipzig: Karl Marx Universität, 1976.

————. "Thomas Müntzer und der Allstedter Bund." In *Täufertum und radikale Reformation im 16. Jahrhundert,* ed. Jean-Georges Rott and Simon L. Verheus, 85–101. Baden-Baden, 1987.

————. "Thomas Müntzers Beziehungen zur Braunschweiger Frühreformation." *Theologische Literaturzeitung* 109 (1984): 636–38.

————. "Thomas Müntzers 'Fürstenpredigt' als Buchbindermaterial." *Theologische Literaturzeitung* 112 (1987): 416–24.

————. "Thomas Müntzers Liedschaffen." *Luther-Jahrbuch* 41 (1974): 45–102.

————. "Thomas Müntzers Weg in den Bauernkrieg." In *Thomas Müntzer, Anfragen an die Theologie und Kirche,* ed. Christoph Demke, 65–85. Berlin: Evangelische Verlagsanstalt, 1977.

————. "Vier neue Müntzerausgaben." *Luther-Jahrbuch* 39 (1972): 110–20.

————. "Die Vorgeschichte von Luthers 'Ein Brief an die Fürsten von Sachsen von dem aufrührerischem Geist.'" *Luther-Jahrbuch* 47 (1980): 40–70.

————. "Zu Müntzers Geburtsjahr." *Luther-Jahrbuch* 36 (1969): 80–83.

Bräuer, Siegfried, and Hans-Jürgen Goertz. "Thomas Müntzer." In *Gestalten der Kirchengeschichte,* ed. Martin Greschat, vol. 5: *Die Reformation I,* 335–52. Stuttgart, Köln, Mainz: Kohlhammer, 1981.

Bräuer, Siegfried, and Helmar Junghans. *Beiträge zur Theologie Thomas Müntzers.* Berlin: Evangelische Verlagsanstalt, 1988.

Bräuer, Siegfried, and Wolfgang Ullmann, eds. *Thomas Müntzers theologische Schriften aus dem Jahr 1523.* 2d ed. Berlin: Evangelische Verlagsanstalt, 1982.

Brock, Peter. *The Political and Social Doctrines of the Unity of the Czech Brethren in the Fifteenth and Early Sixteenth Centuries.* Slavic Printings and Reprintings 11. The Hague: Mouton Press, 1957.

Bubenheimer, Ulrich. "Luthers Stellung zum Aufruhr in Wittenberg 1520–1522 und die frühreformatorischen Wurzeln des landesherrlichen Kirchenregiments." *Zeitschrift der Savigny-Stiftung für Rechtsgeschichte* 102 (1985): 148–214.

————. "Thomas Müntzer." In *Protestantische Profile,* ed. Klaus Scholder and Dieter Kleinmann, 32–46. Königstein, Ts: Athenäum, 1983.

————. "Thomas Müntzer in Braunschweig." Parts 1–2. *Braunschweiger Jahrbuch* 65 (1984): 37–78; 66 (1985): 79–114.

_____. "Thomas Müntzer und der Anfang der Reformation in Braunschweig." *Nederlands Archief voor Kerksgeschiedenis* 65 (1985): 1–30.

_____. "Thomas Müntzers Nachschrift einer Wittenberger Hieronymusvorlesung." *Zeitschrift für Kirchengeschichte* 99 (1988): 228–37.

_____. "Thomas Müntzers Wittenberger Studienzeit." *Zeitschrift für Kirchengeschichte* 99 (1988): 168–211.

Demke, Christoph, ed. *Thomas Müntzer, Anfragen an Theologie und Kirche.* Im Auftrag des Bundes der evangelischen Kirchen der DDR. Berlin: Evangelische Verlagsanstalt, 1977.

Dienst, Karl. "Thomas Müntzer—Eine Gestalt der Bewusstseinsgeschichte." *Luther* (1975): 114–24.

Dismer, Rolf. "Geschichte, Glaube, Revolution. Zur Schriftauslegung Thomas Müntzers." Dissertation, Hamburg University, 1974.

Drucker, Renate, and Bernd Rädiger. "Zu Thomas Müntzers Leipziger Studienzeit." *Wissenschaftliche Zeitschrift Leipzig* 23 (1974): 445–52.

Drummond, Andrew W. "Thomas Müntzer and the Fear of Man." *The Sixteenth Century Journal* 10 (1979): 63–71.

Ebert, Klaus. *Theologie und politisches Handeln. Thomas Müntzer als politisches Modell.* Stuttgart: Kohlhammer, 1973.

Elliger, Walter. *Aussenseiter der Reformation: Thomas Müntzer. Ein Knecht Gottes.* Kleine Vandenhoeck/Ruprecht Reihe. Göttingen: Vandenhoeck & Ruprecht, 1975.

_____. *Thomas Müntzer. Leben und Werk.* Göttingen, W. Ger.: Vandenhoeck & Ruprecht, 1975.

Engels, Friedrich. *Der deutsche Bauernkrieg.* 1850. Reprint. Berlin: Dietz-Verlag, 1955.

Erichson, A. "Strassburger Beiträge zur Geschichte des Marburger Religionsgesprächs," *Zeitschrift für Kirchengeschichte* 4 (1881): 414–36.

Erler, Georg, ed. *Die Matrikel der Universität Leipzig 1409–1559.* 3 vols. Leipzig: Giesecke and Devrient, 1895–1902.

Federer, Jakob G. *Dialektik der Befreiung: eine Studie am Beispiel Thomas Müntzers.* Studien zur Germanistik, Anglistik und Komparatistik 45. Bonn: Bouvier, 1976.

Fischer, Ludwig, ed. *Die lutherischen Pamphlete gegen Thomas Müntzer.* Deutsche Texte 39. Munich: Deutscher Taschenbuch-Verlag; Tübingen: Niemeyer, 1976.

Forell, George W. "Thomas Müntzer: Symbol and Reality," *Dialog* 2 (1963): 12–23.

Förstemann, Carl E., ed. *Neues Urkundenbuch zur Geschichte der evangelischen Kirchenreformation.* Hamburg: Perthes, 1842.

———. "Zur Geschichte des Bauernkrieges im Thüringischen und Mansfeldischen." *Neue Mitteilungen aus dem Gebiet historischer-antiquarischer Forschungen* 12 (1869): 150–244.

Forte, Dieter. *Martin Luther und Thomas Müntzer oder die Einführung der Buchhaltung.* Berlin: Wagenbach, 1971.

Foster, Claude R. "Das Müntzerbild in der amerikanischen Geschichtsschreibung. Ein Überblick auf Grund einiger ausgewählter Werke." In *Der deutsche Bauernkrieg und Thomas Müntzer,* ed. Max Steinmetz, 128–36. Leipzig: Karl Marx Universität, 1976.

Franz, Günther. *Der deutsche Bauernkrieg.* 6th ed., rev. Darmstadt: Wissenschaftliche Buchgesellschaft, 1962.

———. "Die Bildnisse Thomas Müntzers." *Archiv für Kulturgeschichte* 25 (1935): 21–37.

———. "Die Entstehung der 'Zwölf Artikel' der deutschen Bauernschaft." *Archiv für Reformationsgeschichte* 36 (1939): 193–213.

———, ed. *Quellen zur Geschichte des Bauernkrieges.* Ausgewählte Quellen zur Geschichte der Neuzeit. 2d ed. Munich: Oldenburg, 1963.

Friedländer, Ernst, ed. *Ältere Universitätsmatrikel. Universität Frankfurt an der Oder 1506–1648.* Publikationen aus den königlichen Preussischen Staatsarchiven 32. Leipzig: Hirzel, 1887.

Friedmann, Robert. "Thomas Müntzer's Relation to Anabaptism." *The Mennonite Quarterly Review* 31 (1957): 75–87.

Friesen, Abraham. *Reformation and Utopia. The Marxist Interpretation of the Reformation and Its Antecedents.* Veröffentlichungen des Instituts für europäische Geschichte Mainz 71. Wiesbaden: Steiner, 1974.

———. "Thomas Müntzer and the Old Testament." *The Mennonite Quarterly Review* 47 (1973): 5–19.

Fröhlich, Anne-Rose. "Die Einführung der Reformation in Zwickau." *Mitteilungen des Altertumsvereins für Zwickau und Umgebung* 12 (1919): 1–74.

Gerdes, Hayo. *Luthers Streit mit den Schwärmern um das rechte Verständnis Mose.* Göttingen: Göttinger Verlagsanstalt, 1955.

———. "Der Weg des Glaubens bei Müntzer und Luther" *Luther* 26 (1955): 152–65.

Geyer, Iris. *Thomas Müntzer im Bauernkrieg. Analyse zweier seiner wichtigsten Schriften unter Berücksichtigung des sozial- und geistesgeschichtlichen Hintergrunds. Ernst Blochs zeit- und ideologiebedingtes Missverständnis. Thomas Müntzer betreffend.* Bensingheim: Verlag K.H.V., 1982.

Goebke, Hermann. "Neue Forschungen über Thomas Müntzer bis zum Jahre 1520." *Harz-Zeitschrift für den Harzverein* 9 (1957): 1–30.

Goertz, Hans-Jürgen. *Innere und äussere Ordnung in der Theologie Thomas Müntzers.* Studies in the History of Christian Thought 2, ed. Heiko A. Oberman. Leiden, Neth.: Brill, 1967.

_____. "'Lebendiges Wort' und 'totes Ding.' Zum Schriftverständnis Thomas Müntzers im Prager Manifest." *Archiv für Reformationsgeschichte* 67 (1976): 153–78.

_____. "Der Mystiker mit dem Hammer." *Kerygma und Dogma* 20 (1974): 23–53.

_____. "Thomas Müntzer: Revolutionary in a Mystical Spirit." In *Profiles of Radical Reformers. Biographical Sketches from Thomas Müntzer to Paracelsus,* ed. Hans-Jürgen Goertz and Walter Klassen, 29–44. Scottdale, Pa.; Kitchener, Ontario: Herald, 1982.

Goldach, Günter. *Hans Denck und Thomas Müntzer. Ein Vergleich ihrer wesentlichen theologischen Auffassungen. Eine Untersuchung zur Morphologie der Randströmungen der Reformation.* Dissertation, Hamburg University, 1969.

Grane, Leif. "Thomas Müntzer und Martin Luther." In *Bauernkriegsstudien,* ed. Bernd Moeller, 69–97. Schriften des Vereins fur Reformationsgeschichte 189. Gütersloh, W. Ger.: Gerd Mohn, 1975.

Grisar, Hartmann. *Luther.* Trans. E. M. Lamond. 6 vols. St. Louis: Herder & Herder. London: Kegan Paul, Trench, Truebner, 1914–17.

Gritsch, Eric W. "Luther und die Schwärmer: Verworfene Anfechtung? Zum 50. Todesjahr Karl Holls." *Luther* 3 (1976): 105–21.

_____. "Müntzer, Thomas." In *The Encyclopedia of Religion,* ed. Mircea Eliade, 10:156–57. New York: Macmillan; London: Collier Macmillan, 1987.

_____. "Müntzers Glaubensverständnis." In *Der Theologe und Thomas Müntzer,* ed. Siegfried Bräuer and Helmar Junghans. Berlin: Evangelische Verlagsanstalt; Göttingen: Van den Hoeck & Ruprecht, 1989.

_____. *Reformer without a Church. The Life and Thought of Thomas Müntzer (1488?–1525).* Philadelphia: Fortress Press, 1967.

————. "Thomas Müntzer and Luther: A Tragedy of Errors." In *Radical Tendencies in the Reformation. Divergent Perspectives*, ed. Hans J. Hillerbrand, 55–83. Sixteenth Century Essays and Studies 9. Kirksville, Missouri: Sixteenth Century Journal Publishers, 1988.

————. "Thomas Müntzer and the Origins of Protestant Spiritualism." *The Mennonite Quarterly Review* 37 (1963): 172–94.

Held, Wieland. "Der Allstedter Schösser Hans Zeiss und sein Verhältnis zu Thomas Müntzer." *Zeitschift für Geschichtswissenschaft* 35 (1987): 1073–91.

Herte, Adolf. *Die Lutherkommentare des Johannes Cochlaeus.* Religionsgeschichtliche Studien und Texte 33. Münster: Aschendorff, 1935.

Heymann, Frederick G. *George of Bohemia: King of Heretics.* Princeton: Princeton University Press, 1965.

————. "The Hussite-Utraquist Church in the Fifteenth and Sixteenth Centuries." *Archiv für Reformationsgeschichte* 52 (1961): 1–15.

Hillerbrand, Hans J. "The Impatient Revolutionary: Thomas Müntzer." In *A Fellowship of Discontent. The Stories of Five Dissenting Actors in the Great Drama of Church History.* New York, Evanston, London: Harper & Row, 1967.

————. *Thomas Müntzer. A Bibliography.* St. Louis: Bulletin of the Library of the Foundation for Reformation Research 4, 1970.

————. "Thomas Müntzer's Last Tract Against Luther." *The Mennonite Quarterly Review* 38 (1964): 20–36.

Hinrichs, Carl. *Luther und Müntzer. Ihre Auseinandersetzung über Obrigkeit und Widerstandsrecht.* Arbeiten zur Kirchengeschichte 29. Berlin: Walter de Gruyter, 1962.

————, ed. *Thomas Müntzer: Die politischen Schriften mit Kommentar.* Hallesche Monographien 17. Halle: Niemeyer, 1950.

Hoffman, Bengt. *The Theologia Germanica of Martin Luther. Translation, Introduction and Commentary.* The Classics of Western Spirituality. New York: Ramsey; Toronto: Paulist Press, 1980.

Höfler, Karl A. K. von, ed. *Geschichte der hussitischen Bewegung in Böhmen.* Part 1, abteilung 1, vol. 2, *Fontes Rerum Austriacum.* 3 vols. Vienna: Hof und Staatsdruckerei, 1856–66.

Holl, Karl. "Luther und die Schwärmer." In *Gesammelte Aufsätze zur Kirchengeschichte.* 6th ed. 3 vols. Tübingen: Mohr, 1928–32. 1:420–67.

Honemeyer, Karl. "Müntzers Berufung nach Allstedt." *Harz-Zeitschrift für den Harzverein* 16 (1964): 103–11.

——. *Thomas Müntzer und Martin Luther. Ihr Ringen um die Musik des Gottesdienstes. Untersuchungen zum "Deutsch Kirchenampt" 1523.* Berlin: Merseburger, 1974.

Höss, Irmgard. *Georg Spalatin 1484–1545. Ein Leben in der Zeit des Humanismus und der Reformation.* Weimar: Böhlard, 1956.

Hoyer, Siegfried. "Die Zwickauer Storchianer—Vorläufer der Täufer?" *Jahrbuch für Regionalgeschichte* 13 (1986): 60–78.

Husa, Václav. *Thomáš Müntzer a Čechy.* Rospravy Československe Akademie Věd 67, no. 11. Prague, 1957.

Iserloh, Erwin. "Revolution bei Thomas Müntzer. Durchsetzung des Reiches Gottes oder soziale Aktion?" *Historisches Jahrbuch im Auftrag der Görres-Gesellschaft* 92, 2, Halbband (1972): 282–99.

——. "Zur Gestalt und Biographie Thomas Müntzers." *Trier theologische Zeitschrift* 71 (1962): 248–53.

Jordan, Reinhard. "Pfeiffers und Müntzers Zug in das Eichsfeld und die Verwüstung der Klöster und Schlösser." *Zeitschrift des Vereins für thüringische Geschichte und Altertumskunde* 22 (1904): 36–96.

——. *Zur Geschichte der Stadt Mühlhausen in Thüringen 1523–1525.* Beiträge zum Jahresbericht des Gymnasiums in Mühlhausen. 2d ed. Mühlhausen: Dannersche Buchdruckerei, 1908.

Junghans, Helmar. "Ursachen für das Glaubensverständnis Thomas Müntzers 1524." In *Der deutsche Bauernkrieg und Thomas Müntzer,* ed. Max Steinmetz, 143–49. Leipzig: Karl Marx Universität, 1976.

Karant-Nunn, Susan. *Zwickau in Transition, 1500–1547: The Reformation as an Agent of Change.* Columbus, Ohio: Ohio State University Press, 1987.

Kautsky, Karl. *Communism in Central Europe in the Time of the Reformation.* Trans. J. L. and E. G. Mulliken. New York: Russell and Russell, 1959. (German in 1894.)

Kirchner, Hubert, *Johannes Sylvius Egranus.* Berlin: Evangelische Verlagsanstalt, 1961.

Klaassen, Walter. "Hans Hut and Thomas Müntzer." *The Baptist Quarterly* 19 (1962): 209–27.

——. "Spiritualization in the Reformation." *The Mennonite Quarterly Review* 37 (1963): 67–77.

Kolde, Theodor. "Hans Denck und die gottlosen Maler von Nürnberg." *Beiträge zur bayrischen Kirchengeschichte* 8 (1901): 1–32, 49–72.

Kupisch, Karl. "Thomas Müntzer und die deutsche Geschichte." *Luther* 3 (1955): 146–51.

Lau, Franz. "Der Bauernkrieg und das angebliche Ende der lutherischen Reformation als spontane Volksbewegung." *Luther-Jahrbuch* 26 (1957): 109–34.

――――. "Die prophetische Apokalyptik Müntzers und Luthers Absage an die Bauernrevolution." *Beiträge zur historischen und systematischen Theologie.* Gedenkschrift für D. Werner Elert. Berlin: Lutherisches Verlagshaus, 1955, 163–70.

Laube, Adolf, et al., eds. *Flugschriften der frühen Reformationsbewegung 1518–1524.* 2 vols. Berlin: Akademie Verlag; Vaduz: Topos, 1982.

Lefebvre, Joël, ed. *Thomas Müntzer: Ecrites thèologiques et politiques, Lettres choisis.* Lyon: Presses universitet, 1982.

Lexikon für Theologie und Kirche. 2d. ed., rev. 10 vols. Ed. Josef Höfer and Karl Rahner. Freiburg: Herder, 1963.

List, Günther. "Chiliastische Utopie und radikale Reformation. Die Erneuerung der Idee vom tausendjährigen Reich im 16. Jahrhundert." *Humanistische Bibliothek* 1, 14 (Munich, 1973): 129–39.

Lohmann, Annemarie. *Zur geistigen Entwicklung Thomas Müntzers.* Beiträge zur Kulturgeschichte des Mittelalters und der Renaissance 47. Leipzig and Berlin: Teubner, 1931.

Lohse, Bernhard. "Auf dem Wege zu einem neuen Müntzerbild." *Luther* 41 (1970): 120–31.

――――. "Luther und Müntzer." *Luther* 45 (1974): 12–32.

――――. "Thomas Müntzer in marxistischer Sicht." *Luther* 43 (1972): 60–73.

Lortz, Josef. *The Reformation in Germany.* Trans. Ronald Hals. 2 vols. New York and London: Herder, 1968. (German edition 1962.)

Manschreck, Clyde L. *Melanchthon: The Quiet Reformer.* New York and Nashville: Abingdon Press, 1958.

Maron, Gottfried. "Thomas Müntzer als Theologe des Gerichts: das 'Urteil'—ein Schlüsselbegriff seines Denkens." *Zeitschrift für Kirchengeschichte* 83 (1972): 195–225.

――――. "Thomas Müntzer in der Sicht Martin Luthers." *Theologia Viatorum* 12 (1973/74): 71–85.

Mehl, Oskar J. "Müntzer als Liturgiker." *Theologische Literaturzeitung* 76 (1951): 75–78.

Merx, Otto. *Thomas Müntzer und Heinrich Pfeiffer, 1523–1525. Ein Beitrag zur Geschichte des Bauernkrieges in Thüringen.* Göttingen, W. Ger.: Vandenhoeck & Ruprecht, 1889.

Metzger, W. "Müntzeriana." *Thüringisch-sächsische Zeitschrift für Geschichte und Kunst* 16 (1927): 59–78.

Meusel, Alfred. *Thomas Müntzer und seine Zeit. Mit einer Auswahl der Dokumente des deutschen Bauernkrieges.* Berlin: Aufbau Verlag, 1952.

Molnar, Amadeo. "Thomas Müntzer und Böhmen." *Communio Viatorum* 1 (1958): 242–45.

Mueller, Michael. "Auserwählte und Gottlose in der Theologie Thomas Müntzers." Dissertation, Halle University, 1972.

Mueller, Nikolaus. *Die Wittenberger Bewegung.* Leipzig, E. Ger.: Heinsius, 1911.

Mühlhaupt, Erwin. *Luther über Müntzer erläutert und an Thomas Müntzers Schrifttum nachgeprüft.* Witten: Luther-Verlag, 1973.

_____. "Der frühe Luther als Autorität der Radikalen. Zum Luther-Erbe des 'linken Flügels.'" In *Weltwirkung und Reformation. Referate und Diskussionen,* ed. Max Steinmetz and Gerhard Brendler, 1:202–22. 2 vols. Berlin, 1969.

Müller, Lydia. *Der Kommunismus der mährischen Wiedertäufer.* (Schriften des Vereins für Reformationsgeschichte 45, no. 142). Leipzig, E. Ger.: Heinsius, 1927.

Nebe, A. "Geschichte des Schlosses und der Stadt Allstedt." *Harz-Zeitschrift für den Harzverein* 20 (1887): 18–95.

Nipperdey, Thomas. "Theologie und Revolution bei Thomas Müntzer." *Archiv für Reformationsgeschichte* 54 (1963): 145–79.

Oberman, Heiko A. "The Gospel of Social Unrest: 450 Years After the So-Called 'German Peasants' War' of 1525." *Harvard Theological Review* 69 (1976): 103–29.

_____. "Thomas Müntzer: van verontrusting tot verzert." *Kerk en theologie* 24 (1973): 205–14.

Ozment, Steven E. "Thomas Müntzer." In *Mysticism and Dissent. Religious Ideology and Social Protest in the Sixteenth Century,* 61–97. New Haven and London: Yale University Press, 1973.

Preus, James S. *Carlstadt's "Ordinaciones" and Luther's Liberty: A Study of the Wittenberg Movement 1521–22.* Harvard Theological Studies 26. Cambridge, Mass.: Harvard University Press, 1974.

Ranke, Leopold von. *Deutsche Geschichte im Zeitalter der Reformation.* 7th ed. 6 vols. Leipzig: Duncker and Humbolt, 1894.

Rauschenbusch, Walter. "The Zurich Anabaptists and Thomas Müntzer." *The American Journal of Theology* 11 (1905): 91–106.

Rochler, Wolfgang. "Ordnungsbegriff und Gottesgedanke bei Thomas Müntzer." *Zeitschrift für Kirchengeschichte* 85 (1974): 369–82.

Rogge, Joachim. *Der Beitrag des Predigers Jakob Strauss zur frühen Reformationsgeschichte.* Theologische Arbeiten 4. Berlin: Evangelische Verlagsanstalt, 1957.

———. "Müntzers und Luthers Verständnis von der Reformation der Kirche." In *Thomas Müntzer, Anfragen an Theologie und Kirche*, ed. Christoph Demke, 129–38. Berlin: Evangelische Verlagsanstalt, 1977.

———. "Wort und Geist bei Thomas Müntzer." *Zeichen der Zeit* 29 (1975): 129–38.

Rosselini, Jay J. *Thomas Müntzer im deutschen Drama: Verteufelung, Apotheose und Kritik.* Berlin, Frankfurt a.M., Las Vegas: Lang, 1978.

Rupp, Gordon E. "Luther and Thomas Müntzer (1491–1525)." In *The Martin Luther Lectures*, ed. Roland H. Bainton et al., 1:129–46. 5 vols. Decorah, Iowa: Luther College Press, 1957.

———. "Thomas Müntzer." In *Patterns of Reformation*, 157–353. Philadelphia: Fortress Press, 1969.

———. "Thomas Müntzer, Hans Hut and 'The Gospel of All Creatures.' " *Bulletin of the John Rylands Library Manchester* 43 (1961): 492-519.

———. "Thomas Müntzer, Prophet of Radical Christianity." *Bulletin of the John Rylands Library Manchester* 48 (1965/66): 467–87.

Schaub, Marianne. *Müntzer contre Luther. Le droit divin contre l'absolutisme princier.* Paris: Centre National des Lettres, 1984.

Schiewe, Dieter. "Zur Darstellung Thomas Müntzers in vergleichbaren Geschichtsbüchern sozialistischer Länder." In *Der deutsche Bauernkrieg und Thomas Müntzer*, ed. Max Steinmetz, 291–97. Leipzig: Karl Marx Universität, 1976.

Schiff, Otto. "Thomas Müntzer als Prediger in Halle." *Archiv für Reformationsgeschichte* 23 (1926): 287–93.

Schmidt, Martin. "Das Selbstbewusstsein Thomas Müntzers und sein Verhältnis zu Luther. Ein Beitrag zur Frage: War Müntzer Mystiker?" *Theologia Viatorum* 6 (1957/58): 25–41.

Schoch, Max. *Verbi Divini Ministerium I. 1. Verbum, Sprache und Wirklichkeit. Die Auseinandersetzung über Gottes Wort zwischen Martin Luther, Andreas Karlstadt, Thomas Müntzer.* Tübingen: J. C. B. Mohr, 1968.

Schwarz, Reinhard. *Die apokalyptische Theologie Thomas Müntzers und der Taboriten.* Beiträge zur historischen Theologie 55. Tübingen: J. C. B. Mohr, 1977.

———. "Luthers Erscheinen auf dem Wormser Reichstag in der Sicht Thomas Müntzers." In *Der Reichstag zu Worms von 1521, Reichspolitik und Luthersache*, ed. Fritz Reuter, 208–21. Worms, 1971.

Seebass, Gottfried. "Hans Hut, the Suffering Avenger." In *Radical*

Reformers, Biographical Sketches from Thomas Müntzer to Paracelsus, ed. Hans-Jürgen Goertz and Walter Klaassen, 54–61. Scottdale, Pa., Kitchener, Ontario: Herald Press, 1982.

Seidemann. Johann K. *Thomas Müntzer.* Leipzig and Dresden: Arnoldische Buchhandlung, 1842.

Smirin, M. M. *Die Volksreformation des Thomas Müntzer und der grosse deutsche Bauernkrieg.* Trans. Hans Nichtweiss, 2d ed., rev. Berlin: Dietz, 1956.

Sommer, Ernst. *Die Sendung Thomas Müntzers, Taboritentum und Bauernkrieg in Deutschland.* Berlin: Aufbau Verlag, 1948.

Sommerfeld, G. "Der Zwist der Zwickauer Franziskaner mit der Pfarrgeistlichkeit der Stadt Zwickau 1522." *Franziskanische Studien* 8 (1921): 80–84.

Spillmann, Hans O. *Untersuchungen zum Wortschatz in Thomas Müntzers deutschen Schriften.* Quellen und Forschungen zur Sprach- und Kulturgeschichte germanischer Völker NF 41. Berlin and New York: Walter de Gruyter, 1971.

Stayer, James M., and Werner O. Packull. *The Anabaptists and Thomas Müntzer.* Dubuque, Iowa: Kendal-Hunt, 1980.

Steck, Karl G. *Luther und die Schwärmer.* Theologische Studien 44. Zollikon-Zürich: Evangelischer Verlag, 1955.

Steinmetz, Max. *Der deutsche Bauernkrieg und Thomas Müntzer, Ausgewählte Beiträge der wissenschaftlichen Konferenz "Der deutsche Bauernkrieg"—Seine Stellung in der deutschen und europäischen Geschichte. Probleme, Wirkungen, Verpflichtungen.* Leipzig: Karl Marx Universität, 1976.

_____. *Das Müntzerbild von Martin Luther bis Friedrich Engels.* Leipziger Übersetzungen und Abhandlungen zum Mittelalter, Reihe B, 4. Berlin: Deutscher Verlag der Wissenschaften, 1971.

_____. "Schriften und Briefe Thomas Müntzers. Zum Erscheinen einer westdeutschen Müntzer-Gesamtausgabe." *Zeitschrift für Geschichtswissenschaft* 17 (1969): 739–48.

_____. "Thomas Müntzer in der Forschung der Gegenwart." *Zeitschrift für Geschichtswissenschaft* 23 (1975): 665-85.

Straube, Manfred. "Die politischen, ökonomischen und sozialen Verhältnisse des Amts Allstedt in der ersten Hälfte des 16. Jahrhunderts." In *Allstedt—Wirkungsstätte Thomas Müntzers,* 28–44. Allstedt: Rat der Stadt Allstedt, 1975.

Tanaka, Shinzo. "Eine Seite der geistigen Entwicklung Thomas Müntzers in seiner 'lutherischen' Zeit." *Luther-Jahrbuch* 40 (1973): 76–88.

"Thesen über Thomas Müntzer. Zum 500. Geburtstag." *Sonderdruck aus der Zeitschrift für Geschichtswissenschaft* 36 (1988): 99–121.

"Theses Concerning Martin Luther." In *The Luther Quincentenary in the German Democratic Republic 1983*. Panorama, DDR, Auslandspresseagentur. Berlin. 1983.

Thompson, Harrison S. *Czechoslovakia in European History*. Princeton: Princeton University Press, 1953.

Troeltsch, Ernst. *The Social Teaching of the Christian Churches*. Trans. Olive Wyon. 2 vols. New York: Macmillan, 1931.

Ullmann, Wolfgang. "Ordo rerum: Müntzers Randbemerkungen zu Tertullian als Quelle für das Verständnis seiner Theologie." *Theologische Versuche* 7 (1976): 125–40.

Vogler, Günter. "Thomas Müntzer als Student der Viadriana." In *Die Oder-Universität Frankfurt. Beiträge zu ihrer Geschichte*, 243–51. Weimar: Böhlaus Nachfolger, 1983.

Wappler, Paul. *Thomas Müntzer in Zwickau und die "Zwickauer Propheten."* Schriften des Vereins für Reformationsgeschichte 182. 2d ed., rev. Gütersloh, W. Ger.: Gerd Mohn, 1966.

Watterberg, Diedrich. "Der Regenbogen von Frankenhausen am 15. Mai 1525 im Lichte anderer Himmelserscheinungen." *Vorträge und Schriften der Archenhold-Sternwarte Berlin-Treptow* 24. Berlin, 1965.

Wehr, Gerhard, ed. *Thomas Müntzer in Selbstzeugnissen und Bilddokumenten*. Hamburg: Rowohlt Monographien, 1972.

———, ed. *Thomas Müntzer: Schriften und Briefe*. Frankfurt a.M.: Fischer Taschenbuch Verlag, 1973.

Williams, George H. *The Radical Reformation*. Philadelphia: Westminster Press, 1962.

Williams, George H., and Angel M. Mergal, eds. *Spiritual and Anabaptist Writers*. The Library of Christian Classics, vol. 25. Philadelphia: Westminster Press, 1957.

Wiswedel, Walter. "War Thomas Müntzer wirklich der Urheber der grossen Taufbewegung?" *Mühlhäuser Geschichtsblätter* 30 (1929/30): 268–75.

Wohlgast, Eike. *Thomas Müntzer, Ein Verstörer der Ungläubigen. Persönlichkeit und Geschichte*. Göttingen and Zürich: Muster-Schmidt, 1981.

Wolfgramm, Eberhard. "Der Prager Anschlag des Thomas Müntzer in der Leipziger Universitätsbibliothek." *Wissenschaftliche Zeitschrift der Karl Marx Universität* 6 (1956/57): 295–308.

Zuck, Lowell H. "Fecund Problems of Eschatological Hope, Election Proof, and Social Revolt in Thomas Müntzer." In *Reformation*

Studies (Sixteen Essays in Honor of Roland H. Bainton), ed. Franklin H. Littell, 239–50. Richmond, Va.: John Knox Press, 1962.

Zumkeller, Adolar. "Thomas Müntzer—Augustiner?" *Augustiniana* 9 (1959): 380–85.

INDEXES

INDEX

OF NAMES

INDEX
OF SUBJECTS

Authority of, 25, 29, 38, 40, 45,
    79, 112, 116
Gift of, 28, 30, 44, 45, 46, 51, 59,
    72, 78, 82, 89, 113, 114, 115
Holy, 13, 25, 28, 29, 41, 43, 44,
    49, 52, 60, 74, 86, 87, 88, 126
Of Christ, 38, 49, 53, 86
Of the Fear of God, 37, 38, 113
Suffering, 9, 17, 22, 23, 41, 74
    Anfechtung, 37, 41, 45, 53, 60,
    61, 67, 82, 87, 112, 114, 118
Of the Elect, 102
Theology of, 10

Turks, 40, 42, 47, 54, 71, 74, 78,
    102, 112

Twelve Articles of the Peasants,
    97–98, 106

Visions and Dreams, 51, 67–68,
    90, 114

Weimar, Hearing of, 73–74, 75,
    83, 106
Wittenberg Movement, 42
Worms, Edict of, 34, 90
Worship, 6, 14
    Mass, 44, 49, 66
    Reform of, 48–50, 130

Zwickau Prophets, 26, 42, 52, 90